The Photographer's Business Guide

How to take photography from hobby to career, even without a business degree

Janet Howard

Copyright

other than its own or any content available on the Internet that is not created by the author.

Book Cover by Top Book Designer

Contents

Dedicated to all my clients throughout the years.
You've inspired me, supported me, and helped me learn the
lessons I can pass on to others.

To my parents, who taught me I could do anything I wanted in my
life, giving me the courage to envision the life I wanted.

To my cousin, Deb, who sparked the creative fire in me to write.

To Scott, for being so supportive of everything I needed in this
endeavor.

Introduction

Welcome to this emotional and financial rollercoaster called photography! After being in the business for 20 years, I want to tell you all the things I wish I had known when I was starting out and prepare you for what to expect, what to watch for, and how to avoid common mistakes.

This book isn't for everyone, though. I'm going to focus on photography businesses serving clients, specifically geared toward portraits, events and weddings, and products and branding.

This book will:

- Get you prepared for launching and growing your photography business.

- Help you discover systems and processes that can help take your business full time.

- Cover photography-serving clients, such as portraits, weddings, event photography, and corporate brands.

- Share the lessons I've learned from running a photography business for the last 20 years.

- Focus on businesses in the United States. There will be plenty of information that will apply universally, but the details of businesses and taxes are U.S. based.

What this book won't cover:

- Fine artists selling in galleries and art shows.

- The technical aspects of photography. This book assumes you know the basics of how to work your camera and are able to take photos that are worthy of delivering to clients. If you're not at that point yet, you probably aren't ready to start a business. There are a lot of other great resources out there that will help you learn about the technical aspects like aperture, shutter speed, lighting, and technique.

- How to use any specific software. I also won't differentiate between platforms. It doesn't matter to me if you're on Canon or Nikon, PC or Mac.

- Definitive answers. I'll talk about the options and how I do things, but I'm not here to tell you how you "must" do things. (Except for backing up your work, you *must* back up your work). The final decisions are your own to find as an artist and as a business owner. I'm just here to help you ask the right questions. There is no "right" way to do this, and don't let anyone tell you you're doing it wrong.

In this book I'll go through all these elements in hopes of setting you up for success. It's important to keep in mind that this is more art than science. Everything in this book is based on my personal experience, but other people's experience. You might disagree with some things I say, and that's fine. Great, even. Photography is a very personal thing and everyone is going to have their own way of running their business and developing their passions. So take this book as friendly advice, not gospel.

The Workbook

If you'd like more practical ways to work through some of the questions in this book, you'll love the accompanying workbook, The Thriving Photographer's Workbook. In the workbook I take the concepts from each chapter and boil them down to practical activities to help you figure out what this business might look like for you.

Let's Go!

No matter your level of experience or expertise, my goal is to arm you with the knowledge and confidence to transform your passion for photography into a thriving business, unleash your entrepreneurial spirit, and achieve your goals as a professional photographer.

Chapter 1

From Hobby to Business

Should I do this? Can I do this? Is it Time?

Are you loving photography and wondering, "Can I actually make money from this?" Or maybe you're unhappy in your day job and want to take the leap to supporting yourself with something you love.

One of the key indicators that it may be time to turn your photography hobby into a business is when you start receiving requests for your work. It's one thing to get compliments on your photos, but are people willing to pay for them? When friends and family start asking for you to shoot their portraits or weddings, it shows you are producing the quality work that people will pay for.

Especially in the beginning, it's easy to leap into photography wearing rose-colored glasses. This is going to be great! I love photography! I'm gonna be a star! But having realistic expectations is critical.

Let's look at some statistics from Owlguru.com about professional photography:

- Income: Average photographer income in 2021 was $50,290.

- Job Satisfaction: 71%

- 40% say their job helps to make someone's life better.

No matter how passionate you are about photography, is that enough to sustain you through the "business" part of having a photography business? It's not all wedding cake and artistic expression. There is time and effort involved in decidedly less fun stuff, like bookkeeping or marketing yourself, or learning to use new software. Are you willing to not just suffer through those tasks, but actually excel at them? Because no matter how great your photography is, you need to actually be good at running a business.

Turning a hobby into a business also requires financial planning. You'll need to have an accurate idea of your initial investment as well as ongoing monthly expenses. If you ignore the financial requirements, you may end up with a surprise at the end of the first year. Maybe even a surprise big enough that even prevents you from having second year.

Things I Wish I Had Known at the Beginning

1. **You might work 7 days a week.** There is no time off in photography. Unless you're primarily serving business clients, most people want to do their sessions in the evenings or weekends, and weddings, parties and events primarily happen on evenings and weekends. People will

often expect immediate responses. So you need to LOVE what you do, because it can be challenging to maintain a healthy work/life balance. And if you're single, dating people with "regular jobs" can be tricky, since they are usually free on the weekends, when you are working. In addition, you're doing a lot of the customer service yourself, which means responding to calls and emails in a timely fashion, even on the weekends. Working for yourself can feel like working 24/7.

2. **Don't take rejection personally.** Oh my gosh, in the beginning years I just HATED not being chosen. I wanted to know WHY? WHO? What did I do wrong? What I've learned is that photography is really personal, both in style and personalities involved. Some people like a traditional style, some people want to be relaxed, and honestly, as many personalities as there are in the world, they'll all be looking for something different. I can't, and don't *want* to be everything to everyone. Things work best when I really gel with my clients, and that's not something you can force. Now I know that the special connection I have with my clients is what I'm looking for, not getting every job.

3. **It's so much more than photography.** The act of taking photos with my camera is actually a pretty small part of how I spend my time. There's accounting, customer service calls and emails, marketing, networking, equipment maintenance, social media, website development and updates, designing albums, blogging, and troubleshooting random problems. At least half of your photography

business will be *the business of photography.*

4. **You're never done learning.** Photography continually evolves. I'm always trying to learn new things, find new ways to be inspired, and update my techniques. And all while staying current on the latest technology, software options and updates, finding new locations, trying different lighting techniques, and keeping up with current trends.

5. **It's incredibly fulfilling.** I had no idea when I started this journey that it would mean so much to me to share the most memorable times of my clients' lives. I've become like a part of many families, because we share beautiful moments during their engagement, wedding, the birth of their children, birthdays, holidays, graduations, and family reunions. I get to see their happy tears, and hear personal stories about what makes them special. I had no idea how much I'd grow to love some of my clients and look forward to seeing them every year.

The Professional's Mindset

Transitioning from hobbyist to professional is a transformative experience. It requires a shift in mindset. It's essential to understand that photography is not just a creative outlet, but also a business.

It's not about you anymore, you're serving others. That changes the dynamic of the work you produce. It used to be that you'd only have to please yourself with your photos, but now you'll have clients to worry about, and their happiness ultimately determines your success. This changes your focus and delivery. As artists, we can get too personally connected to our work, but when we have clients, we have to realize that they will have feedback and needs of their own, and balancing those two drivers can be a challenge.

Technical Skills: Loving photography isn't enough. You also must have the technical skills to create consistent results. Before you can launch a business, invest time in understanding the technical aspects of photography, like lighting, composition, camera settings, and post-processing techniques. There are hundreds of books, courses, and resources on mastering the technical aspects of photography. Continuous learning and practice will help you refine your skills and elevate the quality of your work.

In the beginning, the best thing you can do is to always be shooting. Keep your camera on you all the time so you get in the habit of noticing what's photo-worthy. You can do this exercise with your phone too, but it's better to use the camera you'll shoot with professionally. The more you use your camera, the less you'll have to think about settings. At this point I can pretty much use muscle memory to change the shutter speed, ISO or aperture on my camera, requiring only a quick glance. The more you have your camera in your hands, the easier it will be to do your job.

Style: In addition to technical skills, you'll develop a unique style that sets you apart from the competition. Your style is your artistic voice and what will attract clients to your work. Experiment with different genres, techniques, and editing styles until you find what resonates with you and your target audience.

I know, with that last one you're saying, "but I'm just starting out, how in the world am I supposed to know what sets me apart?" Or you might even be questioning, "What if *nothing* sets me apart? What if there's not anything special about me?" And I say this: don't sweat it. This is a question you'll continue to explore throughout your career. You don't have to know the answer in the beginning. You just have to pay attention to the question. Having this question in your mind allows you to be continually evaluating possible answers and striving towards finding that thing that sets you apart from the crowd.

You can't *force* your style into existence. You might not know what your style is right now, but it will take shape, I promise. Just by virtue of what you like and what you're driven to create, it will develop. You can have a clue about what your style might be by considering what images really draw you in. What images do you look at and think "Damn, I wish I could create something like that"? Are they emotional? Is the lighting dramatic? Are they framed unconventionally?

Transitioning from hobbyist to professional also requires business acumen. The fact is, a majority of photography businesses fail in the first year or two. Estimates range from 60-85% of them, in fact. What does that tell you?

1. This isn't easy.

2. Lots of people are unprepared for the entirety of a photography business.

3. It's not *just* about photography. There are a lot of elements that go into creating a successful business. In fact, the act

of taking photos may only be about 10-20% of what you spend your time on.

4. There are always outside factors beyond your control, like the economy, trends, or the Covid-19 Pandemic. The successful businesses are the ones that can be flexible, inventive, and adapt to changing situations.

5. You might just decide after a while that photography *isn't* actually what you want to do. You might find the service aspects too trying, or the financial requirements, or the seasonal fluctuations too daunting. You might find that doing this as a job saps the joy you felt when it was a hobby. All of that is ok. It's still a great experience to try it out, and even if you decide against photography as a career, you'll be clear on why it doesn't work for you, rather than always wondering if you could have done it.

Here are just a few of the aspects of a day-to-day photography business in addition to the actual photography:

- Image processing

- Marketing and sales

- Networking

- Client communications

- Portfolio building

- Social Media

- Vendor relations

- Managing contractors and employees

- Maintaining equipment

- Learning new techniques

- Creating and maintaining website

- Location scouting

- Bookkeeping and accounting

- Taxes and licensing

- Scheduling

- Contracts

Now, with this list, there's good news and bad news. The good news: You can outsource many of these things. The bad news: Every single thing you outsource will cost you money and reduce what you income. You'll want to continually evaluate what parts of the business you enjoy, what you hate, what you're great at, and what would be better off in someone else's hands.

Can't I Just Get a Photography Job?

Absolutely! There are plenty of photographers who work full or part time for other companies. There are portrait studios, and photography booking companies that will hire you as an employee and you can get dependable income. You may not even need much experience. But you also probably won't make as much money as a freelancer. In 2024, average rates for photography jobs range from $20 - $28 per hour. The company is going to see most of the income, not you. This may be a good way for some people to jump-start making income from photography. It's also good for people who want to do photography but don't want to have to run a business.

If you want to get photography work without running your own business, you can also seek second-shooting or associate shooting opportunities with other photographer businesses. Many studios offer associate photographer opportunities, where they take on the marketing and business aspects, and all you have to do is show up and shoot. But because they're doing all the legwork, they will also take most of the money, and you'll still be responsible for bringing and maintaining your own equipment out of your cut.

Chapter 2

Getting Ready for Your First Jobs

Ok, you've decided you want to give this thing a try. Let's dive into what you need to do to be ready to get work. I know how artists roll, though. Lots of artists want to skip all the prep work and get to the fun stuff, the artistic stuff. At the end of each section in this chapter, I'll ask the question, *"but what if you don't?"*

Finding Your Niche

It's tempting at the beginning to take any job that comes your way. Wedding? Sure! Real estate photography? Yep! Newborns and families? Sounds fun! I actually recommend trying a little of each of those before you decide on what to focus on. It's the only way to find out what you really want to spend your time doing, and more importantly, what you *don't* want to do. I can't tell you how many times I've had someone assist me at a wedding only to have them realize halfway through the reception they don't want to do weddings. It's fine to try everything, but before you start your business, you should have an idea of what you want to do *and* have a little experience doing it. Why? Because people will usually only buy what they see. If you want to sell your photography, you need to have some of that specific type of photography to show.

Identify your passions and strengths: Start by reflecting on what type of photography brings you the most joy and satisfaction. Is it landscape photography, babies, or headshots? List your strengths and skills, and what you excel at and enjoy. Sometimes what you enjoy and what you're good at might not be the same thing. On the flip side, what do you dislike, or know you don't want to do or aren't good at? Understanding your passions and strengths will help narrow your options and guide you towards your ideal niche.

It's possible you may change your niche at some point. Lots of photographers branch out over time to either expand or reduce the types of photography they do. They might even change niches entirely or move from photography into video.

If you don't define your niche(s): In the beginning, it may be a good idea to try everything so you can see what you do and don't enjoy doing. But as your business progresses, if you don't specialize to some extent, you'll end up doing jobs you don't really want or like, all while having trouble finding the clients you really want.

Assisting/Second Shooting

So how do you get experience if you don't have experience? I recommend for any photographer to start in any niche by assisting, then second shooting. But this can be tricky. Many established photographers don't want to invest time teaching a newbie, only to have them steal their secrets and turn around and become a competitor. Here are some industry-standard things to know.

Do:

- Contact photographers you respect to ask if they are seeking any assistants or second shooters.

- Expect to work a little as an unpaid intern. I know it sucks, but it's part of paying your dues. The first time I work with someone, I usually won't throw them straight into second shooting. I'll add them as an addition to my regular team, so that if their work isn't any good, I haven't lost anything. Because I'm just testing their skills and drive, I don't have a budget for that position. To be honest, most people I hire I only work with once, because either their attitude or the quality of their work doesn't meet my requirements. After that initial "try out", you should expect to be paid for your work unless you are getting an official internship through a school.

- Ask what equipment you need to bring. You'll probably need to bring your own camera, lenses, cards, and even lighting.

- Be on time. No, be early! If someone shows up late to work for me, I won't hire them again.

- Work your butt off. Photographers have a lot on the line with every single client, and the only way you'll get more work is by paying attention and staying on the ball the entire time.

- Pay attention to everything the photographer does. Notice not just what they shoot, but also how they interact with clients, how they manage lighting, and how they set up the shots they need.

- Ask questions, but only at good times. It's fair to ask to see a shot so you can understand the result, or to ask why a photographer set something up in a certain way, but don't interrupt in the middle. Take mental notes of your questions and ask during a break in shooting or after the shoot.

- Be proactive. If you haven't gotten clear direction about what to do, ask what is needed.

- Get a written agreement. It's vital to know what's expected of you and how/when/what you'll be paid. If you're second shooting, you'll also want to spell out whether you can use images you've created for your portfolio, and whose edit you'll use if you do.

Don't:

- Expect to jump right in to paid second shooting. A lot of photographers require you to assist first so they can observe your work ethic, how you interact with clients, and train you to do the job the way they need.

- Address or contact clients outside of the primary

photographer. Allow the primary photographer to handle all communications with the client. Do not contact them after the fact or attempt to give your information to them. When you are working for another photographer, you are the face of *their* business, not yours.

- Use the images you've shot for another photographer in your portfolio or social media unless they have given you express permission in advance.

If you don't want to assist or second shoot: It may be hard to build your portfolio. You'll also do a lot more learning by trial and error rather than picking up best practices from observing.

Educating Yourself

Do you need a degree in photography? Or certifications? Like a lot of things in the photography industry, you might ask ten people and get ten different answers.

In my opinion, a photography degree is great, but not necessary for success in the field. In fact, I often tell people that the most valuable degree for a successful photography career might just be a business degree. There are entire schools of thought on whether artistic skills are inborn or learned, and success or failure in school might not equate to success or failure in business.

However, I'll differentiate the concepts of learning versus education. While a formal education in photography might not be necessary, *learning* is absolutely critical. There are an unlimited number of resources about photography, from TikTok to online forums, webinars, seminars, group classes, and mentorships. Continually learning is a must.

Consider attending photography conferences and events, like Imaging USA or WPPI, or Shutterfest. These are great ways to pack a lot of education into a short period. They also usually include an exhibit hall where you can check out vendors for everything from backgrounds to albums and software. If you're just figuring out what to offer in your business, you'll get tons of ideas.

If you don't want to educate yourself: If you don't have a degree, probably no one will ever notice or ask. If you don't learn about the industry though, you'll be at a competitive disadvantage. This field is packed with people who are continually learning to improve their skills and expand their knowledge. It doesn't mean you won't succeed, but you will be trying to swim with rocks in your pockets.

Certifications and Industry Memberships

There are lots of certifications available for photographers. The PPA (Professional Photographer Association) offers a Certified Professional Photographer program for a reasonable price. Getting the certification might be a good way for you to ensure you've done the prep work to run your business.

In my opinion, certifications only matter to other photographers. I have never had a potential client ask if I had any certification. What it boils down to for most clients is whether they like your work. If they do, they will hire you. They won't know what a certification is or what it means. It doesn't mean you shouldn't get certified, it just means you're doing it for *yourself,* not for your clients.

At the same time, membership in industry associations like the PPA can be very valuable. They are a great source of continuing education and networking with other photographers, and they also offer things like contests if you'd like to enter, as well as insurance options.

Do contests and awards matter? Maybe, maybe not. An award can boost your confidence, for sure. An award can give you recognition within the industry, and might be impressive to some clients. Even your past clients will get a boost if they see you've achieved an award. They might feel proud of you and feel validated about their decision to hire you. But will they notice if you don't have any awards? Probably not.

If you don't get certifications: Honestly, probably nobody will notice.

If you don't belong to industry associations: A few people will notice, but not many. But you'll lose out on benefits for your business and valuable continuing education.

If you don't receive any awards: Probably nobody will notice this either. They'll only notice if you do.

Chapter 3

The Basics of Starting a Business

I'll be honest, this chapter is the least fun and the most necessary in the book. Most creatives want to focus on the creative aspects and don't want to think about the dry stuff like registrations and taxes. Your eyes glaze over and you skip ahead to the next chapter. But as Julia Roberts said in Pretty Woman, "Big mistake. Huge."

This part isn't sexy. It isn't fun. But it's what makes your business a business. A lot of the content in this chapter deals with legal issues, and I am not a lawyer. I can talk to you about my experience, but any actual legal advice about how you implement this for your business needs to come from an attorney.

Business Plans for Photographers

If you ask most photographers about their business plan, they'll answer with one word: "What?"

You know what? Most photographers I know don't have a business plan. Lots of them started a business by the seat of their pants. They got asked to do a shoot, and then another one, and another one, and the business grew organically. They didn't have a plan. But you know what else? Remember that half or more of photography businesses fail in the first year. While a lot of those failures might boil down to people deciding this just isn't the right path for them, a lot are due to a failure to prepare and develop the necessary knowledge and practices.

Unless you're looking for investors or a loan, you most likely don't need a written business plan. But that doesn't mean you shouldn't do it. The exercise of defining what you want this business to be in the broadest sense will help you break down goals into actionable steps and concrete direction. Whether or not you create a written business plan, understanding these elements will increase your chance of success.

1. Define Your Vision and Goals: Start by clearly defining your vision for your photography business. What do you want to achieve? Are you looking to build a successful portrait photography studio or establish yourself as a renowned wedding photographer? Outline your long-term and short-term goals. And it's ok in the beginning to not be sure. But you still need to ask yourself the question.

2. Identify Your Target Market: Understanding your target market is crucial for any business. You can't create an effective message without knowing who you're speaking to and what's important to them. Consider demographics, psychographics, and geographic factors to narrow down

your target audience. This will help you focus your marketing efforts. If you don't have specifics yet, don't worry. It helps in the beginning to take note of the clients you have served in the past and what worked and didn't work with each one. The picture will come more into focus with every job you do, like a Polaroid developing really slowly. At some point you'll work with someone and say, "I wish all my clients were just like her!" And then you'll know.

3. Marketing and Promotion Strategies: Identifying the target market will help you figure out how to reach those people effectively. If your ideal client spends time socializing on Facebook, that's where you need to go. If they love the sleek visuals of Instagram, you'll curate your feed. If they go to wedding shows, you'll get a booth. If they read magazines, you can buy advertising or seek out editorial features. We will explore marketing and promotion in Chapter 8.

4. Market Research: You need to have a good idea of the photography market for your niche in your geographic area. How much competition is there in your niche? How are other photographers pricing their services? Research both established photographers and new ones, so that you can compare businesses like yours and have a sense of where you're going.

5. Pricing and Financial Projections: Pricing in photography is fluid. Your pricing will grow and change as you do. We'll get into how to determine your pricing in Chapter 7, but for now, you can use the market research you used in the

previous step to give a range of what you can be charging.

6. Operational Considerations: This is where you'll look at the day-to-day elements and expenses for your business, including equipment, studio space, and software requirements. At this point, you might not know what those things are, which is why we'll be going through that in upcoming chapters.

Remember, a business plan is a roadmap for your photography business. If you've got people in your life doubting the legitimacy of this new venture, it will help you show that you're serious about making this work. If you do create a written plan, consider it to be a living document, continuously changing as you learn. In the first year it's a good idea to look at the plan quarterly, and then annually afterwards.

If you don't do a formal business plan: Honestly, probably nothing bad will happen. But you might find yourself under-prepared for developing your business.

Your Business Name

I'm talking about this first because when you set up your business accounts and register your business, the very first question is your business name.

There are two basic schools of thought for naming your photography business: naming it after yourself, or coming up with a business name. I've done both, and there are benefits to each option.

Using Your Own Name: The benefits of this are: 1) It's easy. 2) You're always allowed to use your own name for your business, even if it's the same as someone else's name. If you're a single photographer business, people will probably identify you by name anyway, and it creates a personal connection between you and your clients.

Creating a Business Name: This may be the way to go if you aspire to grow the business to include other photographers working with or under you. That way no matter who is shooting on a particular day, your clients will still know the business name.

Once you have an idea or two for your business name, you'll need to see if your business name is available. There are a few places to check:

1. The internet. Just google the name you're considering and see what's out there. This is the simplest way to start because any conflicts will pop up immediately.

2. Check state and federal business registration and trademark databases. Check your state first if that's where you'll be registering. Google "[your state] business name search" and you'll probably find the right spot quickly. Just pay attention to the site: Make sure you are on the site for your state, not imposter sites that want to sell you services. Look at the URL to see if it is a .gov site or a corporate site offering registration services. I'd also recommend checking federally, since an established business even in another state could take issue if your name is the same.
US Patent and Trademark Office: https://www.uspto.gov/

Trademark Search:
https://tmsearch.uspto.gov/search/search-information

3. Do a domain name search to see if there is a domain name available. Even if a business name is available, it can be hard to find a domain name that is both available and desirable. You don't have to have your own domain in the very beginning, but you absolutely will want that eventually. So it's good to know what's available before you go too far down the road with a business name. You can go through any web hosting service to look up possible domain names. Google "check domain name availability" and you'll see tons of options. Once you know your business name and know the URL is available, just go ahead and buy it. It's inexpensive, usually less than $20. And it prevents cyber-squatters from seeing your new business and reserving the name, only so they can sell it back to you for a higher price. Yes, that happens.

If you don't have a business name: You can operate under your own name for an unlimited amount of time. Your name becomes your default DBA (doing business as).

Logo

As for a logo, if you've only taken a few jobs, it's not critical in the very beginning. However, it will go a long way to establish a professional appearance to potential clients. Your logo will visually communicate your brand identity through the colors, style, and fonts you choose.

If you can afford it, the best option is to hire a professional graphic designer to create your logo. A talented designer who specializes in logo design and branding will collaborate with you to get insights into your photography style, target market, and business values to create a unique and memorable logo that reflects your brand's personality.

But if you're not ready to take that leap, there are a ton of free and inexpensive options.

More expensive: I've used for a few logos for clients and the experience was great. You start with some basic style choices and designers submit their creations for you to choose from. You can also try searching for designers on Fiverr.com.

Cheap: Try Etsy, there are tons of logo concepts to choose from at a very low cost.

Free: There are free options from a bunch of sources, including:

Adobe: https://www.adobe.com/express/create/logo

Canva: https://www.canva.com

Once you have a logo, use it consistently across all your marketing materials, including your website, social media profiles, business cards, print advertisements, and email signature. This will help build brand recognition and establish a professional image for your photography business.

If you don't create a logo: Your business won't look as professional as it could. The beauty of a logo is it helps to communicate what kind of photographer you are at a glance, so not having one makes branding yourself and your style a little tougher.

Legal Business Structure

Now you're at a pivotal step. Your business structure carries through the lifetime of your business, and it affects all areas of your business, including taxation, liability, and ownership.

Hang in there! You've found yourself at the least exciting section in this book, but it's also the most important! Don't skip it!

The first step is determining the most suitable business structure. Common business structures for photographers include sole proprietorships, partnerships, limited liability companies (LLCs), and corporations.

If you've taken money for a photography job, you're already a sole proprietor. It just means that you're conducting business as an unincorporated business. It's fine to do that in the beginning, and some businesses continue that way forever. The downside is that you expose all your personal assets to liability from the business because there is no separation between you and your business.

Most photographers create a Single-member LLC. You can choose later to change to a corporation if you grow to a larger scale. You should consult an attorney for help choosing the option that best suits your situation. There are lots of resources available for assisting with the filing or even doing it for you. You can find an attorney in your area or consult businesses who specialize in this. Some options are:

mycorporation.com

legalzoom.com

zenbusiness.com

You can also go to the website for your state's Secretary of State. In some states, the process for registering a business is quick and easy. In other states the process is more complicated, so you might need more help.

The costs of incorporating vary widely state to state, from about $50 to over $4,000. There are often up-front fees when you're establishing your business, plus an annual fee for the lifetime of your business.

If you don't do anything: You'll just be functioning as a sole proprietor, with no liability shield between your business and personal assets.

Taxes

Once you've got your business registered, the next step is working correctly with tax regulations. Don't skip this step! You don't want to get caught on the bad side of the IRS or your state's tax authority. They're not super friendly, and they don't take "I didn't know" as an excuse.

1. **Federal Employer Identification Number (FEIN or EIN):** This is the equivalent to a Social Security Number for a business entity. If you are an LLC or corporation, you must

have an EIN. If you're a sole proprietor, you might not need one, but it's still desirable. Sole proprietors can use their SSN when conducting business, however getting an EIN will give you a layer of protection against identity theft since you won't have to provide your SSN to various vendors and clients. (You'll be surprised how often you need to provide this, especially to corporate clients). You'll also need an EIN if you want to hire employees.

2. **Sales Tax Registration:** Do you need to collect sales tax on photography and products? Probably. Not collecting and remitting sales tax is a common mistake for startup businesses, and it can get you into trouble. In most states, if you sell tangible goods such as prints or albums, you need to charge sales tax and remit it to the state. But recently states have started applying taxes on even digital downloads. For instance, in my home state of Georgia, starting in 2024 they are taxing digital downloads, including photographs and videos. This impacts you because that means that even if you just take photos and send the client an online gallery of finished or raw images, *that product is taxable.* You need to research the rules in your state **before you start selling.** If you can't find clear information about what is taxed in your state, call and ask. Also, since tax laws change, check this out every year. In Georgia, the tax rates for counties and localities may even change multiple times a year. I've made it a habit to call my state taxing authority once a year to make sure I'm handling sales tax appropriately.

3. **Quarterly Estimated Taxes:** As a self-employed photographer, you are responsible for paying your taxes quarterly. If you wait until the end of the year when you file your taxes, you'll have two problems: first, you'll get hit with a pretty large bill. If you've had an hourly or salary job before, think about how much money is taken out for taxes every week, then imagine having to pay it all at once. Second, there is a penalty for not paying quarterly. Keeping up on these taxes is a priority to keeping your business running and knowing how much money you actually have to work with. In the first year it can be hard to estimate how much to pay, but once you file your taxes in the first year, the IRS will actually estimate what you'll have to pay each quarter, assuming your income is stable. If your income is growing quickly, you'll need to re-evaluate this every single quarter. Google It: Quarterly Estimated Tax Calculator.

If you don't get an EIN: You'll be ok if you're a sole proprietor, but your SSN will be used a lot, increasing your chances of identity theft. If you're incorporated, this step is not optional.

If you don't do Sales Tax registration: There are penalties ranging from fines, and possibly even criminal penalties, including jail time.

If you don't pay Estimated Taxes: You'll get a penalty at the end of the year, on top of your already larger tax bill.

State & Local Licensing

Independent of your business formation, your business may need permits and registrations to operate officially in your state, county, or city. For instance, in Georgia, there is an annual business registration for the state, plus you may be required to register your business with the county or city you live in. The only way to know for sure is to look it up in your area. If you skip this step, it's very possible that at some point the city, state or county will find out you've been doing business and send you a notice that you're not complying, along with a fine.

Some specialty niches may also have specific regulations. For instance, some states may require photographers specializing in newborn photography to obtain additional certifications to ensure the safety and well-being of the infants. If you do drone photography, you will probably need to be certified or licensed, and those regulations vary by state.

Remember that licensing requirements may change over time, so you should annually check government websites, professional photography associations, or local business development centers for any changes in licensing requirements and any other legal obligations.

If you don't get the necessary licenses: You may have to pay fines, risk the closure of your business, or even be at risk for criminal penalties.

Business Banking & Finances

You'll need to separate your personal and business finances. This is a must if you're incorporated under any structure, and highly recommended even if you're a sole proprietor.

Opening a dedicated business bank account will allow you to track your income and expenses accurately, making tax preparation and financial analysis much simpler.

Some banks offer specialized accounts for small businesses, providing features like invoicing tools, payment processing, and integration with accounting software. Take time to research different options and select the one that works for you.

If you don't get a business account: It will be harder to do your accounting for your business. If you're incorporated but don't keep your finances separate, you risk losing the liability protections that incorporation affords.

Accounting

Accounting is a boring, frustrating, and utterly crucial aspect of any business. Creatives and accounting often mix like oil and water, but keeping accurate financial records is essential. This means tracking every single invoice, print sale, second-shooter gig, receipt, equipment purchase, software subscription, contractor payments, and even transportation costs, like parking receipts and business mileage for your car. You'll need to keep all your records for several years, as required by federal law.

You have a couple options: Do your own bookkeeping, or hire someone to do it. Most businesses will start with doing it themselves, but if you don't feel comfortable being able to do it right, it's worth the expense to hire someone sooner rather than later.

Personally, I'm a big fan of QuickBooks. I've been using it since my business started. It's easy to use, handles things like sales taxes well, and you can also give your accountant access, so they can access your account to ensure everything is done right. And because there are different versions of QuickBooks for different kinds of businesses, It's available to the smallest of businesses and larger operations. The only downside is the cost, it's not cheap.

With all businesses, understanding the concept of cash flow is important, but especially so for photographers. In most photography niches, income is seasonal. I always joke that I either have a lot of money and no time, or a lot of time and no money. So you'll need to monitor your cash flow so you can anticipate and prepare for the lean times, and for things like quarterly tax payments. It may help to find an accountant who works with photographers and can help give you a heads up to what's coming up in the next month, quarter, and year.

If you don't pay attention to accounting: This isn't optional. You'll need to do it eventually or you'll make your year-end tax filing a frustrating mess. Speaking from experience as someone who has had to go back through a year's worth of mileage records, it is much better to do it a little at a time than to have to spend days or weeks on it later.

Chapter 4
Tools of the Trade

In this chapter, we'll go over all the tools you need to get through your day to day business. We'll look at the costs involved, and how to make do until you can afford the ultimate solution for you.

For each element we look at in this chapter, I'll suggest the long-term goals (which will be more expensive) as well as some "make do" options that are lower cost or even free.

Cameras and Gear

You've picked an expensive profession, my friend. A photographer is never done buying gear. Never. In the beginning it's about building up what you need, then it's about improving the quality of your work. Then multiply that by the desire to have to have the newest, coolest technology. Oh yeah, and throw in a side order of having to replace equipment that fails.

Let's look at the key gear and equipment you need to consider when building your photography business, focusing on the niches of portraits, events, products and wedding photography.

Cameras:

It all starts with a high-quality camera. Your niche might determine the features you'll need in your camera. Wedding photographers often need excellent low-light performance and dual card slots. Sports photographers will prioritize speed.

Since switching platforms is expensive, whatever you start with, whether it's Canon or Nikon or Sony, might be where you stay for quite a while. Switching involves replacing not just the camera, but all your lenses, so do some research before you invest in equipment to with the goal that it will be able to grow with you for several years.

Lenses:

You'll need a range of lenses. Some niches might only require a few lenses, and others (like weddings) might call for a greater variety of lenses.

Architecture & real estate: Wide angle (14-35mm)

Portraits: Standard/portrait (35-85mm)

Products: Standard/portrait (35-85mm), macro

Sports: Telephoto (135+)

Weddings: Wide angle, standard/portrait, telephoto, macro

The most equipment you'll need is for weddings, since you'll need to capture a mixture of grand scenes, portraits, and intimate closeups. You may also be more restricted in the distance you have to maintain from your subjects, especially in churches.

When you're choosing lenses, quality is better than quantity. If you're trying to create great images, having low-quality lenses can hold you back from creating the images you desire. One good-quality professional lens is probably better than 3 cheap "kit" lenses.

Zoom or Prime?

Whether you need zoom or prime lenses depends on what kind of photography you'll do and what's important to you. Here are some comparisons between them:

Flexibility: Zooms are more flexible and easy to shoot things like weddings or sports, where subjects are constantly moving and might be unpredictable. With fixed length prime lenses, I always say I "zoom with my feet", moving myself to get the framing I want rather than zooming with the lens.

Aperture: Most primes offer wider apertures, which are great for low light. Zoom lenses will usually be higher apertures, 2.8-4.0 or above.

Size and Weight: Primes tend to be lighter than zooms. Wide aperture lenses (under 1.8) can also get heavy.

Sharpness and Quality: Traditionally, zoom lenses are more prone to distortion and chromatic aberration, although many newer lenses are exceptions to the rule. Photographers who prefer prime lenses often say they offer greater sharpness and more pleasing bokeh, especially at lower apertures.

Lighting:

This varies a lot depending on the type of photography you'll be doing. If you're planning to shoot entirely outdoors using only natural light, you might not need much, but most photographers will want to be able to work under a variety of lighting conditions or create the light they desire. There are a multitude of options when it comes to lighting equipment, from flashes and continuous lighting to softboxes, diffusers, and reflectors, And the selections change all the time. Throughout your career, you'll want to experiment with lighting techniques that will give you the look you want. Light is the basis of good photography, so never stop experimenting and learning lighting techniques and tools.

Special Considerations for Wedding Photography:

Be prepared to bring TWO of EVERYTHING. Never show up to a wedding with only one camera, one lens, one memory card, one flash, one *anything*. I say this with a great deal of certainty: at some point, every piece of equipment will fail or get broken. It has happened to me personally. I've had a camera fail, a lens break, a memory card get corrupted, a flash die, and batteries mysteriously drain, all in the middle of a wedding day (thankfully not the *same* wedding day). Imagine you're shooting a wedding and suddenly your equipment fails and you have no backup. From that point forward you can't capture anything, letting down your clients on the most important day of their lives.

Every single point of failure you allow may mean that you can't deliver what you've promised. A client not getting the images they've dreamed of their entire lives is the makings of social media posts that go viral, and the end of careers. If you can't afford a backup camera, borrow one or rent one for the day. Add it in to the cost of your services. Your backup camera doesn't have to be the same model or same quality as your main camera. However, you should be familiar with the model or have it be as close as possible to the model of your main camera. Attempting to figure out a new camera amidst a hectic day is a recipe for disaster.

Supplies:

The costs don't end with big-ticket items. You'll need accessories such as memory cards, extra batteries, camera bags, and cleaning kits. It might not seem like much, but it's an essential part of your gear, and a lot of these items need to be replaced regularly. Memory cards may need to be replaced every 2-5 years depending on how much use they get.

Long-Term Goal: A full set of gear including cameras, lenses, lighting, and supplies, with backups for every piece of gear. Total costs can range from $2,000-$15,000+.

Make Do: Rent or borrow what you need for each gig. You'll spend less upfront, but the costs will add up fast, so once you know you need something on a recurring basis, re-invest your profits back into your business to get equipment one piece at a time. Keep a prioritized list of what you need next and how much it costs.

Computers and Software

There are plenty of hobbyist photographers who can get by editing in free software on their iPad. But the more volume you have, the greater the processing power you need.

Laptop v. Desktop

You might be fine in the beginning editing images on your laptop or even a tablet. For myself, I have a laptop that I work on if I need to work remotely, but I only edit images on it if absolutely necessary. The more pixels you have to work with, the better, so image editing can be tougher on a small laptop screen. My preferred setup is a desktop system with two 27-inch monitors. That way I can devote one entire monitor to the intricacies of photo editing, and have a second monitor for emails, web browsing, accounting or other tasks. Desktops are also better in terms of speed. Most desktop configurations will give you more memory, more hard drive space, and faster processors. Processing speed and memory become crucial in image editing, so upgrading your computer may save a lot of time, just in processing speed.

Long Term goal: a dual-monitor desktop system, maxed out on processor speed, memory, and hard drive space.

Make Do: a laptop or even a tablet.

Monitor Calibration

In my opinion, every professional photographer should calibrate their monitor. Calibration ensures that the colors you're seeing on your monitor will match what your clients see in their prints, albums, and proofs. Calibration tools are available from $150-$300. It's good practice to re-calibrate every month or so, since display qualities can shift over time. In the past, I've been lazy about re-calibrating, especially when I'm really busy, and I have noticed the color shift.

Long Term goal: Monitor calibrator tool. You should be able to buy one and use it for years.

Make Do: You'll be fine for a little while without one, but if you're regularly doing prints or other products, or if you notice that your prints or online images don't match what you see on your computer, you'll want to get a calibration tool.

Image editing tools

No matter how great a camera you have, your images aren't complete until you edit them. The industry standard is the Adobe Suite, which is available to photographers at an affordable monthly price. The learning curve can be steep, particularly with advanced editing in Photoshop, but there are an abundance of online courses available.

There are also thousands of presets available for Lightroom and actions for Photoshop to speed up your processing and give you consistent looks. Presets range from classic to trendy, and from free to hundreds of dollars. Presets can be a great way to streamline your editing and create consistent results, but you also risk your photos looking just like every other photographer who uses those same presets.

In addition to the standard tools, there is also niche-specific image editing software, tailored for portrait and wedding photographers. These tools often offer specialized features such as skin retouching, makeup enhancement, and background replacement. Software like PortraitPro, Topaz Labs Retouch Ai, Portraiture and On1's Portrait AI offer ways to do advanced edits quickly and easily.

Outsourcing is an option preferred by a lot of photographers. Since image editing may end up being 50% or more of the total time you spend in your business, many photographers choose to outsource it completely so they can prioritize shooting, which actually produces income. Outsourcing can be expensive though, so it needs to be a decision that your finances can support.

A less expensive option to outsourcing is AI Editing. I can say the best thing I did for my business in 2023 was to start using AI editing. It allowed me to use my same editing style but cut out 60% or more of the time it takes to edit a shoot. As of this writing, the leader is ImagenAI, but since AI is changing so quickly, I suspect by the time this book makes it to your doorstep there will be other options emerging.

Long Term goal: A collection of editing tools to cover all your needs, including retouching, and AI automations to make the job go faster. You may also consider outsourcing editing entirely.

Make Do: There are plenty of inexpensive software options available. Many photographers function using Lightroom and/or Photoshop alone for the entirety of their business. Use free tutorials and YouTube videos to learn skills.

Whether you choose to use Adobe Photoshop, Lightroom, or other web-based tools, remember that image editing is a skill that requires practice and experimentation. Take advantage of tutorials, online courses, and communities to learn new techniques and stay updated with the latest trends in image editing.

Image Storage and Backups

If there's one thing you take away from this book, please let it be this: BACKUP YOUR FILES. I need to write it in all caps because it's so crucial. I see panicked posts on a way too regular basis from photographers, begging for resources for how to recover files that haven't been backed up. Don't let this be you!

Over my twenty years in photography, I've had every single thing fail at some point. Memory cards fail. Hard drives fail. In fact, hard drives fail way more frequently than I'm comfortable with.

Camera Dual Card Slots:

The backups start at the second you take an image. Early in my career, I was shooting a wedding and my memory card became corrupted. Luckily it happened early in the day, so the only images I lost were from the preparation. I learned a very valuable lesson that day. Memory cards can and will get corrupted at a random time and for no reason at all. If what had happened to me had been at the end of the day instead of the beginning, I might have had to refund all the client's money, and would have had to live with the fact that they had no photo memories of their day. I've seen that happen to other photographers. From that point on, I made sure that I only shoot weddings on a camera with two memory cards, writing to both cards at the same time for an instant backup.

Make Do: If you're shooting portraits, you might be ok with a single card slot. For weddings, I don't recommend it.

Hard Drives:

I have a 3-part backup system. Some would say it's overkill, but I assure you I have a personal story behind every level of backup. (I'm telling you, electronics fail!) My personal system is set up like this:

1. **Two Working drives** that contain everything I'm working on currently. I fill up a 4TB hard drive every 6-8 months. This is one drive that contains all the raw files, Lightroom catalogs, and final jpegs for every project. Plus, a backup of the working drive that backs up nightly. That way if a drive fails, the worst-case scenario is I'm out one day's work.

2. **Archive drives**. Once I fill up a working drive, I move only the final Jpegs to an archive drive. This is also accompanied by a backup drive, which is backed up nightly.

3. **Offsite/Cloud backup.** I currently use BackBlaze to do an

off-site copy daily. It keeps a copy of both my working drives and my archive drive. Because despite your best efforts to back up in your home/office, things can happen. You could get robbed, there could be a flood or fire, who knows. And as tragic as those events are, they'd be compounded by the tragedy of losing ALL your clients' images. In the early days when I couldn't do a cloud backup, I'd have an additional hard drive that I'd take to a secondary location at a friend's house for an off-site copy. Luckily, now you can do a cloud backup for less than it would cost to buy a second hard drive, and without the bother of continually updating it. Yay technology!

4. **Online galleries** (a/k/a Bonus backup!) I also use my online gallery provider as an offsite backup. Since I use it to provide files to clients and I pay for unlimited storage, this has become an additional offline backup for me.

Make Do: You're just starting out and you don't have the resources to buy a ton of hard drives or keep a cloud backup. Here's what you can do: Use the hard drive on your computer as one working drive, and use TimeMachine to make a cloud backup. Then you've at least got two copies, one off-site, for a reasonable price.

Backup Software:

If you're on a Mac, Time Machine is a perfectly fine, free option. You can specify what to back up and how often. I personally use Carbon Copy Cloner for my nightly backups because of its reliability and flexibility. Either way, you'll want to use a backup/cloning software instead of just copying files from one drive to another, for two reasons. First, cloning software does more than just copy files, it checks for errors. Second, cloning software can verify that specific folders match (including removing files), rather than just blindly copying.

Make Do: If you're not ready to invest in backup software, TimeMachine will probably work fine.

On Keeping Files:

Once you've completed processing a shoot, you have a few options for handling the files:

1. Maintain all the files for a specified amount of time and then delete them. (Saves the most hard drive space)

2. Delete all the raw files after you deliver the final gallery of jpegs. Keep only the final jpegs for the images you deliver.

3. Delete the raw files for the unused images. Keep the raw files and jpegs for the images you deliver.

4. Keep everything, all the raw files and the final jpegs.

This is a matter of preference as well as finance. Most photographers choose option 2 or 3, because it conserves hard drive space while still maintaining old files.

You certainly have the option of only keeping your files for a specified amount of time (maybe 6 months or a year) and then deleting them. Lots of photographers do that. But I can tell you that if you're in this business for a while, at some point you'll have a client come back years later wanting to access their images. I've had a couple who never bought an album come back for their 10th wedding anniversary to buy an album when their kids started asking why they didn't have one. I've had a couple whose home got destroyed in a fire hoping to purchase a replacement wedding album. Sure, I could have turned them away if my contract only required me to keep their images for a year, but I was thrilled to be able to serve those clients years later, especially when it meant their memories otherwise would have been lost forever.

Raw files can be huge, so getting rid of them makes sense. But … I'm in the minority here, but I don't ever delete my raw files, even the ones that don't make the final gallery. First of all, I've deleted too much stuff by accident, so I try to just leave my working drives untouched to avoid the accidental deletion of necessary files. But there's another reason.

True story. A client calls me well after the wedding, maybe six months to a year … they say their grandparent has just passed and they were wondering if I had any more photos of them from the wedding. I went through the original raws to find one more lone photo. It was a good shot of the grandparent, but I hadn't put it in the gallery because the bride was also in the photo and she looked terrible in it. So I cropped in on the grandparent and gave it to the bride, explaining why I didn't use the photo in the first place. She was super grateful to have the additional image of her loved one. Being able to provide that to them at such a difficult time brought me a lot of joy. That scenario or something like it has happened to me a few of times through the years. It would be way cheaper in conserving hard drive space to get rid of those files, but the satisfaction that I get from knowing I could go back is worth it to me.

If you choose option 3, you'll only keep the raw files for the images you deliver, which gives you the ability to go back at some point and re-process the images. This year I'm going on 20 years in the business, which means one of my first clients has a daughter graduating high school. I thought it would be fun to pull up old photos and compare her newborn session to graduation. Fun, right? Well, listen, no matter how great you think your photos are right now, if you make it 20 years and have to look back at your early work, you just might cringe. It might even happen after five years. Maybe it's a really dated editing style, or the lighting, or just your general skill level. You'll learn a lot over time and looking at your past work can be cringe-worthy. So anyway, there I was, wanting to do a retrospective, but I didn't want to show the edits I had originally done, I wanted to update them. That meant I had to go back to the raw file. I was glad to have it!

Another reason for keeping the raw files is that files can get corrupted. No matter how many backups you have of a particular image, if the original gets corrupted, all your backups will also be corrupted. Murphy's Law says that if you're under the gun and need one file from a job and there's only one corrupted file on the drive, those will be the same. (It's happened to me!) If you keep the original raw files, you'll at least be able to find the original and re-create the edits.

Make Do: In the beginning, hard drives can be a big investment. If you need to conserve hard drive space, you can certainly remove the raw files from your drive as soon as you deliver the gallery. Heck, if you don't care about the stories I told, you might be fine getting rid of all the files after your promised time. You'll use up a lot less hard drive space than I do. It's up to you how you run your business.

Pro Tip:

Don't reformat memory cards until you've delivered the final product. More than once I've been editing a job, and it occurred to me that there are files missing. "Wait, I remember taking an image of the bride holding a donut. Where is it?" Well, remember above how I talked about how backups are better than file copying? Sometimes files don't get copied, because there was a glitch or the drive disconnected or the power went out, whatever. It's not common, but it happens. While editing, I realized there were a bunch of files missing. If I had overwritten that card, I might not be able to recover them. That means that you'll need a lot more cards though, since you might have other shoots to complete before you're finished editing.

Make Do: If you don't have enough memory cards to avoid over-writing cards before you finish editing, just don't blindly reformat without double checking the files. At least compare the total number of files on the card and the number of files in the folder on your working drive to verify they match before you erase anything.

Image Delivery

How you deliver images to clients can enhance your brand. The way you choose to do this directly affects your clients. The image gallery should look professional, be aesthetically pleasing, and functional.

There are a bazillion gallery systems out there, at a wide range of prices and functionality. I won't evaluate them in depth because their functionality and pricing changes monthly. But I can give you some potential options to consider and offer suggestions on how to evaluate which one is for you.

10 Popular photo delivery systems:

- ShootProof

- Pixieset

- Zenfolio

- Flickr

- Dropbox

- CloudSpot

- Pixpa

- SmugMug

- Pixellu

- Pic-time

What works best for me might not work for you. Here are the criteria I used to figure out the best option:

- Is it pretty? This is probably the most vital one for me. I want my clients to have a great experience looking at their galleries.

- Can I brand it? When people look at the gallery, does it say "Dropbox", or my company name? Can I use my logo, my colors, and my fonts to make it look like the rest of my website and materials?

- What are the storage limits? Can I start small and work up to larger storage limits or unlimited storage as my business grows?

- What's the pricing plan? Do I need to pay a lot all at once or can I start at smaller levels and work up to more storage? Can I pay a smaller amount monthly or do I need to pay for an entire year up front?

- Are there time limits on how long a gallery can remain active? If yes, do I feel comfortable telling my clients they have to make decisions and order or download their images within a certain time?

- Can my clients order prints and albums from their gallery? If so, do I need to pay a commission/processing fee for those images? And if so, can it communicate with my accounting software?

- Does the interface, including viewing, downloading, and ordering, provide a good user experience? Is it easy for people to navigate and figure out how to do what they need? Even older relatives who may not be tech-savvy?

- Does it interface with my other apps or offer other functionality, like studio management/CRM and website creation?

Make Do: Until you can invest in a gallery system, you can use Dropbox or WeTransfer. You may not have much space for free though, so you may have to give your client a short amount of time to download the files, after which you delete them to make space for the next shoot.

On Raw Files:

There's a big debate among photographers about whether to give your client RAW files. Should you only give them select finished, edited images, or hand over all the unedited files to the client?

For the most part the answer is probably no, you shouldn't give a client all the raw, unedited files, for a few reasons:

1. Part of your job as a professional is to create a finished product to give to your client. Handing over unedited files is like going to a pizza restaurant and having them hand you a ball of dough and some toppings you have to cut up yourself. It's very different than the final product.

2. The raw files kind of suck. They're flat. They're not cropped the way your final images will be. They include all the blinks, ugly expressions, and the lighting tests you did of your own team. They simply are not a professional product.

3. Many people won't have software to deal with RAW files.

4. If you're sending out unedited files, you can't really develop a signature style. Let's look at a scenario: You give your RAW files to a client. They edit them all in a style you hate, it's hideous. Then they post the images, crediting you. Now you've got a bunch of people thinking this is the style you'll create, and you're horrified by it. This scenario, unfortunately, is not rare.

5. If you're not culling and editing, your clients can use any unusable frame or misfire as an example of your work. It's not uncommon for me to accidentally click the shutter as I'm moving around, resulting in a blurry image of the floor. I also might take a test shot just to see the light, not caring if it's in focus. I've seen that kind of outtake photos used against a photographer as an example of their incompetence.

There are some exceptions to the rule. A corporate client or two has required raw files because they have a distinct editing style they need to match. And for some events that get promoted live, I've given raw files to a corporate client so they can get an image out to the press or social media while I'm still working.

Contracts

It's essential from the beginning to have good contracts. This details the expectations of who is responsible for what and when, and what happens if something goes wrong.

You might think "But I'm just doing small jobs for family right now, I don't need a contract." I'm going to argue that contracts are necessary *especially* with family and friends. Because family can be the most likely to make incorrect assumptions about what you'll do for them, and be demanding about getting what they want. Your family dynamics introduce an entirely new wrinkle into the already challenging area of client relations. Your non-family clients aren't going to call your mom to complain about your attitude. They're not going to ruin Thanksgiving because they're still mad about what they thought you were going to deliver even though you never said you would. If they're paying you, even family members need a contract to outline exactly what they're getting and when, *before* the first click of the shutter. And it sets an important tone. It says you're serious about what you're doing.

Unless you're starting your new photography venture in the evenings after your day job as an attorney, don't write a contract yourself. Eventually you may have an attorney draft your own contract, but in the meantime, there are plenty of free and inexpensive contract templates available. Even Etsy has lawyer-approved inexpensive contracts, and a quick Google search will give you a variety of options to download and use instantly.

One size contracts don't fit all. The contract you use will differ based on the kind of photography you're doing. I have different contracts for weddings, portraits, corporate branding or products, or fashion/editorial. Your contracts need to be specific for the genre of work you'll do and the type of clients you'll serve.

Make do: If you don't have a lot of money to invest, search for free photography contract templates, or consider buying one from Etsy, for as low as a few dollars.

Customer Relationship Management (CRM)

As your business grows, you'll want something to help keep track of all your shoots and communications. A CRM can help you gather information, keep relevant documents, and automate tasks and workflows. Basically, spending less time on administrative tasks and more time on actual photography.

There are practically endless options out there, at a variety of prices and functionalities. I feel like I've tried all of them by now, and they all have pros and cons. You may not need or want your CRM to do everything, so here are some of the primary features you'll look for:

- Contracts. Most CRMs will allow you to send contracts and get e-signatures.

- Invoices. This is different for photographers than a lot of businesses. Most other business will have invoices due in 15, 30, or 60 days. But photographers need to be able to auto-schedule due dates based on the date of your shoot, so that you can ensure you're paid when your contract says the payments are due.

- Calendar management. CRMs can automatically block off time in your calendar when a shoot is booked and alert you if you're in danger of double-booking.

- Payments. Some CRMs will enable your client to pay with credit cards, bank drafts, or third party apps like PayPal.

- Scheduling. My life got so much easier the day I started

letting my clients do automated bookings. They can check my calendar, book, sign a contract, and pay a retainer all at the same time, eliminating the back and forth of trying to find time in everyone's calendar.

- Questionnaires. You'll find questionnaires helpful for everything from getting a sense of someone's style before they book, to getting scheduling details for a wedding, to asking for feedback after a shoot.

- Automations. You may be able to automate your workflow elements, such as sending out questionnaires before or after a shoot, payment reminders, and other messaging. If your calendar is filling up, getting those routine tasks off your plate is a godsend.

- Workflow. Some CRMs will even allow you to manage your task flow, giving you to-do items as they occur. You might want reminders of when your image delivery is due for your sessions, or trigger one to-do item when another is completed. For instance, as soon as you deliver a gallery, you might want the system to trigger a to-do item for you to create their album.

- Client portals. This is a helpful feature for your clients, where they can log in and see everything that pertains to you in one place, including contracts, questionnaires, and invoices coming due.

Make do: Until you can afford a full CRM system, you can do all the functions yourself. You'll just need to keep really good notes on deadlines and when to follow up with clients.

Insurance

Yes, you need insurance. A lot of new photographers don't think this applies to them, but here's what you need and why it matters.

Liability Insurance:

This covers you in case there is a loss or injury to a person caused by you or your staff, like if a piece of equipment falls over and hits someone, or if your equipment overheats and starts a fire. It also covers you in case you're unable to provide services you've contracted to complete. If you're working on-site at venues, many of them will require proof of liability insurance before they'll allow you on the premises. Sometimes I don't get informed of this restriction until a day or two before an event, so if I didn't have insurance I'd be taking the chance of losing the job and disappointing my client right before the shoot.

Equipment Insurance:

Can you afford to replace all your equipment if it gets stolen? You might have $10,000-$20,000 or more invested in cameras, lenses, lighting, and more.

A lot of photographers make the mistake of thinking their equipment is automatically covered under their homeowners/renters or auto insurance. It might be, but it might not. The only way to know is to call your insurance agent and ask (or read your policy). In some cases, your insurer will require any equipment used for business to be on a separate policy.

And if you're traveling with your gear, like to weddings or events, you may need a special policy called Inland Marine. Many auto insurance policies won't cover the full value of your equipment if it's stolen from your car, so call your agent to find out if you're covered and what additional coverage you might need in case of a theft or other loss.

You can try asking your current insurance agent (from your car or homeowners policy) if they can give discounts for additional policies.

Make do: You can put off getting insurance for a little while if you have enough money to replace your equipment or if you're covered by your other home or auto policies.

Studio and Meeting Space

Do you need a studio space? It depends on what kind of photography you'll be doing. If you'll be doing a lot of portrait or product photography you might need it. Your studio requirements will depend a lot on the niche and look you want to focus on. The problem is that renting a studio can be quite expensive, and you'll need to have a steady income to support it. And rent isn't the only cost. If you want your own studio, you'll also need to furnish it with backgrounds, furniture, props, and lighting equipment. It can be a lot to take on.

Luckily, if your goal is to work in a studio full time, but you need to ramp up, there are a few options that allow you to work in a studio without breaking the bank.

Mobile Studios. All you need to create a "studio" is a background and lighting. There was a time when I had rolls of seamless paper and canvas backdrops that I'd transport to any location. This is particularly good for corporate headshots, since you can bring the studio to the client and they don't need to get their entire office out to another location. All you need is a few backdrops in various colors, stands for hanging them, and a couple lights, either flash or continuous.

Home Studios. When I first started out, I designated a room in my basement as a photo studio. We had a couple rolls of seamless paper for backgrounds and a few lights, and it had a separate entrance so people didn't have to walk through our home. You don't need to have a lot of space for it to work, just one room that you can clear of furniture so you have space to work. Then you'll invest in the backgrounds, chairs/stools and any props you'll need, depending on the clients you're serving. You'll need to check any regulations for your neighborhood, since some Home Owner's Associations or apartment complexes have restrictions on running a business out of your home that draws members of the public.

Hourly Rentals. Peerspace.com is a great way to find studios you can rent by the day or by the hour. You can find everything from plain seamless backdrops to full production sets. Many hourly rentals also offer lighting equipment or assistance if you don't have the gear yourself. In Atlanta, there is a set to suit just about any look a client is going for, but in other cities you may find that there's not as much variety. Hourly rentals are a great way to offer studio settings without the high overhead of a monthly rent payment. When I need studio space for a session, this is what I do, adding the rental fee to the cost of the session. I even try to schedule studio sessions on the same day so that I can just do one afternoon or daily rental and schedule sessions back to back to make the most of my time there.

Shared Studios. It is becoming more common for multiple photographers to share a studio space. This allows you to access a studio regularly without having to bear the cost all by yourself. Look for other photographers in your area who might already have a studio space they can share. You'll want to create an agreement that specifies exactly how many hours of studio time you get per month and have a good way to schedule so that everyone can easily see the calendar.

Meeting Space. I remember the days when I'd meet potential clients at Starbucks. For the cost of a cup of albeit expensive coffee, I could meet my clients to talk about their wedding photography. It wasn't ideal, because I'd occasionally have to jockey for position in a crowded space or try to talk over the roaring coffee grinder, but it worked. Today, post-Covid, I rarely meet people in person, instead favoring video chats. If you do want to meet in person, either for potential client meetings or for in-person sales, there are so many meeting spaces available, including private conference rooms, from co-working companies like WeWork, Spaces, and others.

Make do: Most photographers will be fine without a studio in the beginning. You can shoot on-site, and use hourly rentals when you need them. As you grow, you can move from hourly rentals to shared spaces, before finally creating your own studio.

Chapter 5

Workflow

Let's look at what workflow looks like, from the moment a client inquires to them walking away happy and excited about the next time they get to work with you.

Pre-shoot

1. **The inquiry.** Someone finds you and reaches out to inquire. Yay! Respond as quickly as possible. Be friendly. Ask questions about what they want and make yourself available for questions. There is an entire art to how to best respond to inquiries to increase your chances of booking.

2. **Meeting/discussion.** You'll come up with a process that works best for you, whether it's meeting in person, chatting on the phone, exchanging emails, or just sending a price guide. This is your chance to show them why it's a great idea to hire you and make all your pricing and processes clear. Every client should know all these things before they decide to book:

- Price, including any retainer required to hold the date,

when the balance is due, and any post-shoot per-image costs.

- Timeline for when they can expect to receive their images.

- Any restrictions you have, such as limits on the number of locations, outfits, or individuals involved in the session. If there are additional fees for mileage, additional people or outfit changes, specify them now.

- The number of images they can expect to get. They should know both how many they'll be able to choose from, and how many final edited images they can choose.

- The image delivery process. They need to know if they will receive an online gallery, or if you'll conduct an in-person or online sales session.

- What they should expect to receive. Are they fully edited images? Will they be web size or full-size images, or prints only? And will they be watermarked?

1. **The booking.** Yay! They've booked you! Every one of my bookings includes these three elements:

- A contract.

- A questionnaire. This lets me know things like how many people will be involved in the session, how many outfits they're planning, the location, any special needs, and any questions or requirements they have.

- A retainer. Their session isn't booked until they pay a

retainer to hold the date. I will also give them the ability to pay in full at the time of booking, and to add a tip if they like.

1. **Planning.** Leading up to the session, a little prep work goes a long way.

- **Check Your Calendar.** Confirm the shoot time and place are in your calendar. If this isn't automated by a CRM, double check your calendar to be sure it's correct. You may also want to put any deadlines in your calendar for getting payments or delivering images.

- **Scout Locations.** Sometimes a client needs help with choosing a location. You may need to go out to scout locations or choose a studio, or arrange for permission to shoot at any private locations. Some popular spots like botanical gardens or other popular photo locations may require a fee, so inform your client if there are any fees involved.

- **Create a Shot List.** Find out what the client wants the end result to be and create a list of must-get shots. If there are more than a few, write them down and bring it with you so you don't forget.

- **Send a Pre-Shoot Questionnaire.** For larger events or weddings, you'll want to gather detailed information including a list of important people, the schedule, and a list of vendors. I'll also ask for their social media tags or event-specific hashtags so I can tag them when I post.

The Shoot (and Payment)

1. **24-48 hours out:** Call, text or email the client to confirm time and place. Check the weather forecast. Confirm with your client where on-site you'll need to meet up, and where to park. If your shoot is outdoors and you're expecting weather challenges, be prepared to reschedule or come up with an alternate location.

2. **The night before:** Get your gear ready. Make a list of what you need to bring and check it off as you pack it in your bag. Include backups of cards and batteries. Check that batteries are fully charged. Make sure you have successfully downloaded everything on the cards you plan to use, then format them so they are empty at the beginning of a shoot. A common beginner mistake is to bring used cards to a shoot and either mistakenly overwrite them or not have enough room to shoot the entire session.

3. **Arrive early.** Find out exactly how long it will take you to get to your destination. Don't guess. Don't *think* you know how long it will take. Check the time the night before or morning of, and then check it again an hour or two before, just in case traffic situations cause the expected trip time to change. I can't tell you how often people show up late because they thought they knew where they were going, only to find out it's going to take 30-60 minutes longer than they thought. Arrive on site early enough that you can get set up and be ready to click the shutter at the session start

time.

4. **Shoot.** Check in with your client throughout the session so you know they're happy and getting the shots they want. And have fun!

5. **Get paid.** Collect your final payment from your client, according to the contract terms, whether it's before the shoot or after.

6. **Put deadlines in your calendar.** If you have a CRM, you may be able to keep an automated task list with deadlines. If not, just put them in your calendar so you're always aware of the deadlines you have coming up.

7. **Send a Thank You.** The day after the session, thank your clients & remind them of what to expect, like when they'll see the images and the next steps.

Editing

There's no right answer to editing. You'll find the process that works best for you. But here's what mine looks like. I do my editing in Lightroom, so your process might work differently if you use Photoshop or other software.

1. **Download and back up.** Download the images from your camera's card to your computer. Before you go any further, back them up yourself (or set up an automated backup). I recommend using the same file structure for every shoot. For instance, I create a folder for every shoot, and inside that folder are three more folders, for Raw Files, Lightroom

Catalog, and the final images.

2. **Create a Lightroom catalog.** I create a new Lightroom catalog for every session.

3. **Import the images into Lightroom.**

4. **Culling** (First pass). Here's where you'll decide which images you'll work on, and which get tossed. There are a couple ways to approach this.

Culling Considerations

"Editing Out": When you "edit out", you'll remove the images that are obvious rejects and work on everything else. This usually results in more total images you'll work on. If you're editing out in Lightroom, you'll probably mark the bad images as "reject."

"Editing in". When you "edit in" you're going to select just the images you want to work on. This usually means looking through the images to find similar ones and only choosing one or two in a group of similar images. I used to edit out and switched to editing in because I felt like it resulted in less overall work. I choose to flag my images that I'm keeping, but others rank them with stars.

AI Culling. There are software options like FilterPixel, Narrative Select, AfterShoot, and Imagen-AI, that will do the culling for you. They can be helpful for quickly identifying images that are out of focus, or with eyes closed. As of this writing, I personally don't think AI editing is good enough to set and forget. You'll probably still have to do some manual culling. But you might find that it saves you time.

5. **Sneak peeks.** If you want to provide quick sneak peeks to clients, you can insert a step here, even before the initial edit, where you'll choose a few favorites to do a quick edit and send to your client. Sneak peeks can get your client excited and have something to show while they wait for the full gallery. Not all photographers do them, and you can decide if it works for you. I usually don't, although sometimes when I'm doing my initial cull I'll see an image I'm excited about and want to share it right away.

6. **The initial edit** (Second pass). Once I've selected the images to work on, I go through each image individually and adjust the exposure, contrast, saturation, temperature and tint, curves, clarity, and more. Here is where you'll apply presets if you use them, doing any additional edits to each image to perfect it. You can also bring any images into Photoshop for additional refining. Once I've gone through all the images once, I usually try to put the images away for a day or more to work on something else. Sometimes when I come back to view them with fresh eyes, I discover I want to make changes. *AI Editing:* This is the best change I've recently made to my workflow. Now instead of my initial edit, I use ImagenAI to do it for me. I uploaded thousands of images to Imagen to allow it to learn my style, and now I just create the Lightroom catalog, flag the images I want to use, and it does the first edit for me. While there is additional expense involved, the time savings are incredible. Not only does AI editing replace the most time-consuming step, but it means I don't need to take time away from the images to

look at them fresh.

7. **Refining** (Third pass). This time I look at the images in grid view so I can see how they relate to each other. I can see if the color and other settings are consistent across images, and get an overall view of the entire collection as my client will see it. I'll make final adjustments to images as needed.

8. **Rename images**. This is an optional step, but I feel like it's a much more client-friendly experience to have the images renamed. I use a standard naming convention, their name + an image number. It allows us to easily find the images if they're ordering prints or selecting images for retouching. An additional benefit is that your client can't look at the image numbers and look for gaps, indicating how many images didn't get used for the final gallery. (Yes, I've had clients look through images and say "How come it went from JHS2004 to JHS2008? Where are 5, 6, and 7?"

9. **Export**. I export final Jpegs into a sub-folder in the shoot's main folder.

10. **Deliver Images.** This will depend on the method you choose:

- For all-inclusive sessions, upload the images to an online gallery and send it to your clients. Specify how long the gallery will be online and what they can do with the images, including downloading files, or ordering prints.

- For IPS sessions, schedule a time with your client to go over their images. At this meeting (in person or online), show them their images and choose on site which ones your clients will want to order, what products they want (like prints, frames, canvas or metal prints) and what sizes. With IPS, there will be an additional step of producing and delivering the products your client has ordered.

Post-Delivery

1. **Back up final image files.** Once the editing is done, I can back up the final images to my archive, where they are also backed up to the cloud. If you choose to delete the unused raw files (or all raw files) this is when you'd do it.

2. **Format cards.** Once you've completed a shoot, you can format the cards and get them ready to use again. I have a set of small drawers next to my desk and I keep all the used cards in one drawer and all the formatted cards in another drawer. That way I'm not scrounging through cards at the last minute to try to find an empty card I can use when I'm preparing for a shoot.

3. **Bookkeeping.** My CRM (HoneyBook) interfaces with Quickbooks so I don't have to enter every new invoice and payment. But before I had that timesaving feature, I entered the invoice and the payment in QuickBooks as soon as it was complete.

4. **Social media posts.** I do my social media posts in batches, so I'll select the images I want to use and schedule them to go out at future dates. Don't forget to tag your clients (if they want you to) and any vendors whose work can be

seen in your images.

5. **Provide images to vendors.** I sometimes create separate galleries for vendors I work with a lot so that I can curate the images that they will want to show and create a central location for all their images.

6. **Blog.** If you hate writing, sure, you can just show images. I personally like telling stories about what's special about my clients, and it can give a behind-the-scenes perspective. I also write about any venues or vendors involved and use keywords to make them more visible through search engines.

7. **Send questionnaire and get reviews.** After a session I send a review questionnaire so I can track how things are going. And when they rate 5 stars, I ask if they would write a referral, which I can put on my website or blog or other social media, or give them links where they can post a review online.

Chapter 6

Building Your Reputation from the Beginning

"Whenever I'm about to do something, I think, "Would an idiot do that?" And if they would, I do not do that thing." - Dwight Schrute

Don't let your reputation be something that just happens to you by accident. You can actively create it from the beginning by being intentional about your actions.

Communicating Effectively

No matter how great your photos are, poor communication can kill a business. That includes what you say, who you say it to, how you say it, when you say it, and when you need to not say anything. Outside of your photos, this is the bulk of your client's experience with you. Let's look at each of these aspects of communicating.

What You Say:

It's essential to communicate details about what your client can expect and when. Be clear about times and places for meetings and shoots. When in doubt, spell it out. I also recommend clear written communication that you can go back to if there's a misunderstanding. Even if you have a verbal conversation with someone, recap it via email or text to verify that what you said and what they heard are the same thing.

Who You Say it To:

Your clients are part of your communication in a shoot, but other people will also ask you for things. Be polite and accommodating, but never forget who your client is. It isn't uncommon to get direction from someone that conflicts with what your client wants. For example, I remember a wedding where there had been a contentious divorce between the groom's parents. The groom wanted to get a photo with both his parents, but his father didn't want to be in the same photo as his ex. We quickly arranged the photo and took it, and afterwards the father came up to me and demanded I delete the photo. I told him I wouldn't because his son was my client and his son wanted the photo. My loyalty was to my client, so if another person's request differs, they need to work it out between them.

With weddings in particular, there can be a lot of conflicting needs, particularly when a parent pays for the wedding. For that reason, many photographers will only contract with the bride and groom and not the parents. I personally don't have that restriction, however I make it clear that my loyalty is to whoever signs the contract. Who pays the bill is none of my business.

You may also have conflicting requests from guests at weddings and parties. At one wedding, the crowd got a little rowdy and my photos reflected it. Afterwards, I got a call from a guest who was embarrassed by her actions in some of the photos, demanding I take the photos down. I told her I would need to check with the couple, since they are my clients. So I contacted the clients and they agreed that I could remove the photos from their gallery. I wouldn't ever make that decision without consulting the client first.

How You Say It:

Particularly with weddings and portraits, your demeanor and delivery are a big part of your client experience. I can't tell you how many horror stories I've heard from clients about weddings they attended where the photographer was loud, pushy, demanding, rude, or generally off-putting. When that happens, people will tell the story to their friends for *years.* So be friendly and personable. Make it a point to create a personal connection with your clients. Try to appreciate them as individuals. With photography we have a unique opportunity to make people feel seen and beautiful and appreciated in ways that most people don't experience. Treat your clients like friends. Look for what's special about them and *tell them*. Be genuine and authentic in your words and praise. People will know if you're bullshitting them.

Be polite, kind, and friendly, even when you don't feel like it. A photographer deals with people constantly, and you can be absolutely sure that some of those people are going to be annoying, demanding, condescending buttheads. Your manner of communication should not change when you're dealing with one of those people. As I always say:

Someone else's bad behavior does not justify your own bad behavior.

In times of conflict (and make no mistake, no matter how hard you try, it will happen), If you don't feel like you can be kind in the moment, just wait. Listen to your client's issues and tell them you'll get back to them. Take time to cool off and think clearly about what you want to say. Don't communicate anything until you can do it with kindness and empathy for their situation, even if you know in your heart that they are wrong and you are right.

Let's say you're having a dispute with a client. The client is wrong and you're right. You're so right, you're the rightest you've ever been. Nobody has ever been as right as you are now. Here's what you need to know: *Nobody cares if you're right.* Yep, you heard me. The only person who cares if you're right is you. What will matter more than who is right or wrong will be how you resolve the conflict. It's how you reach a resolution that will stay in the mind of your client.

That doesn't mean giving in to what the client wants if you don't want to. It just means approaching the situation with kindness and a genuine desire to create a resolution that works for both of you.

Be personable, establish a connection, and treat each client as an individual. This will not only make the experience enjoyable for your clients, it will also lead to positive referrals, which are invaluable for growing your business.

When You Say It:

Responding to people promptly tells them you're on the ball and competent. I strive to respond to every single message as quickly as possible, measuring in minutes, not days. I love it when I can respond instantly to a client and take them by surprise that they get an answer so quickly. But while that's the rule, here are two exceptions:

1. **Work/Life balance.** I don't suggest checking messages all through the night. You wouldn't think it would happen, but I do have clients who will call, text or email on weekends and in the middle of the night. I'm fine with that, which is why I set my do-not-disturb hours in the evening. You'll want to set healthy limits from the beginning about when you need time for yourself.

2. **While you're with clients.** The only time I'm *not* checking messages is while I'm actively serving a client. Your client needs to know that in the hour(s) you'll spend with them, you are fully present. That means no checking email, no taking or making calls, no sending texts. Your phone should be on silent and should not be in your hand at any moment during a shoot. That way you can communicate to your client that they are valued and appreciated.

Everyone works differently, and some people prefer to batch tasks throughout the day. If that's your style, that's fine. Just make sure you respond to all your messages at least three times a day: first thing in the morning, mid-day, and at the end of the day. Whatever schedule you work out, do it consistently. The longest someone should wait for a response is 24 hours.

When You Need to Just listen:

Communication goes both ways. It's not just about speaking to your clients, it's also about listening to them. You need to know beforehand what your client wants to get out of a session to know whether you can deliver it. Ask lots of questions about your client's needs and goals, both before you agree to do a job and during the shoot. Afterwards, follow up with them to get feedback about how it went so you can make adjustments if you need to. Making your clients feel heard and valued sets you up for long-term success and ensures your clients will return over and over.

Rocking Your Deadlines

Deadlines are promises. That means you need to know *before* you make promises how long it will take you to do something, whether it's delivering a gallery, designing an album, or even answering questions. If you're not sure, overestimate the time you'll need. Under-promise and over-deliver whenever you can. If you get a reputation for blowing off your deadlines, that's an easy way to tank your business before it even gets started.

As you get more experience, you'll get more accurate at estimating the time it will take you to deliver, but I still recommend adding a little buffer time to your estimates, just in case. At this point in my career, I take about two weeks to turn around a wedding, but my contracts promise three-week delivery. Because no matter how good you get at estimating timelines, sometimes life will get in the way of your plans. You might get sick, take a vacation, get overwhelmed with work or suffer some other crisis. Life happens, and it's a part of your deadlines. You can't tell clients you'll make your deadlines except when you don't. And when you don't make a deadline, it tells your client that they're not a priority for your business, making them less likely to return. Even if you're great about meeting deadlines, there will be a time when something has to slip. Maybe you landed in the hospital, or your computer died, or some other totally unforeseen circumstance is going to get in the way of you meeting your deadlines. It will happen at some point. When it does, you need to do these two things:

1. **Communicate early and often with your client.** Let them know as soon as possible that there's an obstacle preventing you from fulfilling your promise to them. Do not wait until the deadline has passed, and don't wait for them to reach out to you first. Be clear about what's happening and what you're doing to deal with it.

2. **Come up with a Plan B.** What actions are you going to take to deal with what has happened? You can't be passive. You need to be proactive about coming up with alternative solutions. Almost anything can be outsourced. While it might be more expensive than your normal workflow, you might need to take a short-term financial hit in order to deliver consistent results. In these cases, the long-term value to your business isn't spending a few more dollars to get you through an issue, it's making sure that your clients know you can deal with adversity professionally. As you make adjustments and new plans, communicate with your client every step of the way.

Developing a Signature Style

"Signature Style." Words that can strike fear in the heart of a new photographer. You're being told over and over that it's so key to set yourself apart from the crowd, yet every time you hear those words, you get an uneasy feeling in the pit of your belly. What's my style? How do I define it?

In the early days, I'd be interviewing with a potential client and they would ask me to define my style, and it was like my world would move in slow motion. Words would fail me and I'd sit there not knowing what to say, and hoping the pause wasn't as long as it felt. Of all the questions I could answer, I didn't know how to define myself to others.

I used to love experimenting with styles. I was kind of a preset junkie, getting new presets all the time and changing with every shift of the wind. When I delivered a gallery, I'd deliver some images in color, some images with a stylistic treatment, and some in black and white, and I might make adjustments to each session depending on my "artistic vision". I loved the creativity. But what I thought was creative expression was translated into unpredictability. Potential clients weren't sure what to expect, and I was losing business I wanted. I had to figure out a way to be consistent in my style so my clients could feel confident that they know what they are going to receive at the point they decide to hire me.

Eventually, your style will take shape purely by the body of work you deliver. In the meantime, you can look at what you love and what you *want* to create.

Let's start with what appeals to you. The images that you're drawn to as a viewer are probably also going to be the kind of thing you'll be energized by creating. Do you like images that are:

- Candid or posed?

- Black and white or color? And within color, there are different editing styles: true color, dark and moody, light and airy, textured.

- Trendy or classic? There are trends in photography. At one point it was aged images, with textures and yellow tones. There was a phase where magazines were dominated by dark images with overt orange tones and very little green. Right now direct flash is a big trend. These trends come and go, and you'll have to decide if you want to embrace trends, go with a classic look, or create your own style. Personally, I've done the trendy thing, and honestly I cringe when I look back at my trendy phases, because they look very dated quickly. On the plus side though, trends often gather a wide following, so it can be easier to get business with a trend that is in vogue.

- Natural light or artificial light? Do you want to work in a studio where you can control everything, or work outdoors in nature?

- Lifestyle or traditional? For family photos and headshots, do you like shooting in a studio, or do you want to see people in their every day environment, making dinner together, playing games, and showing the activity of daily life?

Consistency and Growth:

There are conflicting drivers of any photography business. How do you both stay consistent in your delivery *and* continue to grow and evolve your work? It's a question of simultaneously changing and staying the same. It helps to check in with yourself regularly. What are you enjoying? What are you proud of? Are you bored or excited? Continuing to ask yourself questions will help you strengthen your business and your style and ensure you're happy with continuing your business this long term.

Looking Professional

You're going to make a lot of first impressions as a photographer, and they are all valuable. You will interact with every client, as well as guests at weddings and events, models, assistants, corporate employees and more. With each one of those interactions, you will project an image and create a brand, including not only your product (the photos) but also your communication, and even your personal style. Every interaction you have with people becomes part of your "brand", and many of the non-client people you encounter at shoots will become clients in the future if they enjoy the experience of working with you.

Dress for Success. One thing that says "amateur" in loud flashing neon colors is dressing inappropriately or too casually for an event. Particularly for weddings, don't show up in shorts or jeans. Don't wear clothing that's too sexy or attention-grabbing. Find out the dress code for the event and dress in a way that fits in with the other people in the room. My goal is to dress at the same general level as guests. I should look like I fit in and just happen to have a camera. I'll dress professionally for corporate shoots, more casual for family shoots.

For weddings in particular, the hardest part of building your wardrobe is finding good comfortable shoes. With a lot of photography you'll be on your feet for 8 or 10 hours at a time. A quality pair of comfortable shoes with good support is one of the best investments you can make. And if you can find a pair that's not ugly, you've found the holy grail.

Chapter 7

Pricing and Packaging Your Services

I f you want to start a heated argument between a bunch of photographers, bring up pricing strategy. There are different schools of thought on the topic. But you know what? This is *your* business. You can do things however you want. No matter what price you end up with, there are a few ways to approach it.

Market Research

We touched on market research in Chapter 1, but let's dig a little deeper.

Whether or not you do a business plan, it is worthwhile to do market research. Without it, you're just walking around blindfolded. But there are a couple kinds of research to do: on customers and competition.

Customer research

The good news is, there is a lot of research at your disposal. PPA and other organizations do annual surveys, covering topics like client expectations, budgets, and services. Reading these survey results will help you see trends and identify any gaps in the market that you can use to differentiate yourself. You can also join online forums, social media groups, and photography communities to hear what others are experiencing in your niche and in your city. If you have your own questions, you can also ask your clients about what helped make their decision and what problems they encountered. If they take time to help you out, show your gratitude with a gift card or some free prints from one of their sessions.

Competitor research

Research your competitors. You can find out how they market themselves, price their services, what they deliver with their packages, and what makes them special. Not to copy them, but use what you find as an example of what you want and don't want for your own business. If you find everyone is doing something one way and you want to do it differently, do it! It might just give you an advantage over the crowd.

Do's and Don'ts of Competitor Research:

Do:

- Visit photographer websites, Instagram feeds, magazines and promotional materials.

- Look at pricing. Notice how they structure their packages and their services. Is their pricing based on packages or a la carte?

- Pay attention to style and content. What is the difference in presentation between a high-end photographer in your area and a budget-friendly photographer, as far as image quality, design, and the tone of their written communication?

Don't:

- Don't call or email a photographer pretending to be a potential client. Not only is it disrespectful of their time, it messes up their sales funnel. You'll learn that every time you get an inquiry you feel hopeful about the booking, and you can get disappointed when they ghost you. When someone pretends to be a client, it throws off your income expectations, and can be just a bummer.

- Don't call a photographer expecting free advice. Even if a photographer is helpful, it's not their job to educate you. Be responsible for your own knowledge.

- Don't copy a competitor's pricing or marketing exactly. Not just because it might be copyrighted and unethical, which it is, but because in a lot of markets it's beneficial to have professional and friendly relationships with other vendors, including other photographers. Plus, how can you differentiate yourself if you're a clone of someone else's marketing?

Should I Shoot for Free (or Cheap)?

Lots of established photographers get their knickers in a twist when they see newbie photographers working for free or very cheap. These photographers believe that low-priced photographers undercutting prices is a danger to the industry, and that new photographers should price themselves consistent with the established photographers around them.

I might get hate from some of those people for saying this, but I disagree. I think those responses come from a place of fear. After all, the only way to compete against low prices is to be *better.* That puts the pressure on *me.* That's a scary place to be if I'm not secure in my ability to be better than the new, low-priced competition.

I think in general there is an assumption among consumers that a new photographer is going to be less expensive. Some people shop for photographers as if they're going to a garage sale. They're hoping that among the board games with missing pieces and the stained children's clothing they'll find that rare vintage vase, that extraordinary find that they buy for $1 only to find out that it's worth a million. It's a gamble. They're willing to take a chance, hoping they'll find that rare fantastic photographer who is underpriced only because they need experience. But with the garage sale approach, you also might get what you pay for.

Just last week, I was asked to provide a quote for a party. When the potential client saw my price, they got sticker shock. They were planning to pay about a quarter of what I quoted. But when I dug deeper, it turns out that last year at the same event they had paid hardly anything, and the pictures they received were terrible. So while it took them a while to adjust to the new price, they ended up deciding to pay what I was asking. And afterwards they were so happy they vowed to call me for their next event. At that point, they understood the price difference because they had made a losing bet the first time.

When photographers complain about low-priced newcomers, the mistake they are making is that they assume that all photographic services are equal, and they just aren't. When someone hires a photographer, they're not just paying for someone to show up with a camera. They're paying for quality, experience, service, delivery, and reliability. A new photographer, no matter how talented you are, just doesn't have the experience, reputation, and business acumen yet. And that's not an insult, it's just the cycle that we all go through. At the beginning of your photographic career, you might know how to take photographs, but you're just figuring out the rest of it. You haven't had personal experience yet with all the ups and downs and issues and solutions that make for a seasoned professional. Even if you're talented, you're still more of a gamble.

So it's natural to shoot for cheap when you're starting out. After all, if you're experimenting with different types of photography, a lower price is a great way to get the job. The fact is, there's a lot of photography work out there. There's work at low rates, and there's work at high rates.

As a beginner photographer, getting the experience, finding your style and preferred niches, and developing your portfolio may be a higher priority than being able to generate full-time income. That's ok. And it's equally ok for the people with smaller budgets to seek photographers with lower prices. There's something for everyone out there.

Shooting for free can open doors to networking opportunities and collaborations with other industry professionals. It allows you to grow your network and gain valuable connections. I've done many shoots for other vendors as a professional courtesy, and some of those relationships have followed me throughout my last 20 years in the industry.

However (and it's a big however), it is important to know your worth. Charging lower prices is a temporary means to an end. It's an investment in your business, much like paying for education is an investment. It's an initial investment, not a career strategy.

Early in my career, my prices were low. In 2004, I think I did some weddings for $600. At that price, you get volume. Lots and lots of people can and will pay lower prices for photography. But volume is dangerous for photographers. What comes with volume is being overwhelmed, burning out, and risking not being able to make deadlines. It's a short-term solution. There was a time when I did 50+ weddings a year, sometimes 3 in one weekend. And I'll never do it again. The amount I had to work to churn out all those images by the promised deadlines meant I had no free time. I felt exhausted all the time. This kind of overwhelm kills a lot of photography careers just as they get started. When your prices are low, you might want to outsource to keep up, yet you'll have no money to do it. Lots of photographers go through this phase of business only to find they've been working for minimum wage or less.

The answer is periodically raising your prices to reflect your improved levels of experience and quality.

So back to the question: Should you work for free or cheap? Maybe, but for as short a time as possible. In the first year or two, you may want to evaluate your pricing on a quarterly basis.

There's one last aspect to this: the dreaded photos-for-exposure proposition. If your photography is good, you'll get people approaching you to say they have this great "opportunity". They'll say they have tons of followers and if you do this work for free, you'll get tons of exposure. Most likely, these people are taking advantage of you. I've worked with a lot of celebrities and influencers, and often they don't even credit their vendors. They are serving *their* brand, not yours. If someone approaches you with a job like that, evaluate it like this: If it's the kind of shoot that you want to do and you can't see another way to get it, go ahead, but expect *nothing*. Consider whether it's something you'd do for free anyway. But most people will only do that kind of thing once and end up regretting it.

In conclusion, shooting for free can be a strategic tool for photographers wanting to create or grow a business. It can help build a strong portfolio, establish connections, and gain exposure in specific niches of photography. However, it is essential to approach this decision with careful consideration, setting clear boundaries, and understanding that it is a stepping stone rather than a long-term business model. By doing so, you can harness the power of shooting for free to propel your journey from hobbyist to professional photographer.

Pricing Methods

Pricing is a science and an art. There are a ton of resources out there, and honestly you could read entire books on this one topic. I highly recommend the courses offered by the PPA, because they will teach you detailed methods for determining your pricing. There are three ways to consider your price, and the best solution is to use all of them to come up with pricing that is unique to you and your situation.

1. Value-based Pricing: This means pricing your services based on the value you bring to the table, reflecting your unique skills, expertise, and experience.

2. Cost-based Pricing: This method starts with calculating the total cost of delivering your services and then adding what you need to profit. This can be an eye-opening exercise, because so many photographers think they're doing great, only to find out that their expenses are killing them. The costs of doing business include upfront expenses like your cameras, gear, computers, hard drives and supplies. It also includes overhead like office supplies, studio rentals, insurance, advertising, marketing, gas and parking, internet and phone. Don't forget about all the seemingly small monthly fees, like software subscriptions, backup solutions, online gallery fees, CRM & contract systems. Each of those might only cost $10 a month, but they add up fast. You might well find that you have to do a couple of sessions per month just to break even, before you even make a dollar of profit. Once you know all of your

expenses, you can add on top of that what you need to make, allowing for what you'll pay in income tax.

3. Competitive Pricing: If you've done your market research, you know what your competitors' prices are, so you can certainly start with a price that equates to your value in the market. The limitation of this method is you only have half the information you need. You don't know what your competitor's costs are. What if you're pricing yourself the same as your closest competitor, but their expenses are half of yours? So while you can use your competition as a factor in your pricing, it doesn't stand alone as an actual pricing method.

Sales Strategy: To IPS or Not to IPS

There are two kinds of photographer pricing strategy:

IPS ("In Person Sales") or Per Image Pricing

IPS-based photographers charge a session fee, and then charge per image (digital or print). Usually that means going through the session with the client to determine how many images they want, and what products they want, whether it's prints, wall art, albums or digital files. The client receives personal service in the delivery phase for each session.

Pros:

- There's an opportunity for huge sales from any shoot. Since people pay per image, if they love a lot of images, you could generate phenomenal sales.

- IPS sales typically involve fewer total images, which means less editing work.

- You control how your work is displayed.

- It's a more personal experience between photographer and client, which could translate into loyalty to your company.

- You have options in how to price and present your products. You can do a la carte single-image pricing, or offer packages of images. Package pricing can entice customers to buy more to get additional discounts.

Cons:

- It's more time consuming. Some IPS meetings can take several hours, and scheduling the meeting might not be a priority for some clients.

- You need to feel comfortable doing sales. If you love sales, this could become a pro rather than a con.

- You need to invest in samples of each product. People buy what they see, so if you want to sell things like canvases, framed prints, or metal prints, you need to have an example to show your clients.

- You need a place to meet. If you decide to have your own studio, that's great, because you'll have a place to meet that has all of your product samples. If not, you'll need to lug the samples to your meeting place or customer's home, which can be cumbersome.

- While there is a huge upside, there is also less guaranteed income per session.

- Some clients can be tempted to steal photos through screenshots rather than pay per-image fees.

- Vendor offerings change frequently, which means having to recalculate your prices or get new samples as their offerings change.

If you choose the IPS method, the fundamental element is to communicate clearly with all your clients and potential clients. The worst thing that can happen is for a client to get surprised by unexpected costs. Before potential clients book a session, let them know how the fees are structured and what the post-session costs and average spend is.

All-Inclusive Pricing

With all-inclusive sessions, you charge a session fee and clients can download any or all of the images you put in the gallery at no additional charge.

Pros:

- Clients know up-front exactly what they're going to spend, no surprise costs after the fact.

- You don't have to do "sales" if you're not comfortable with it.

- You don't have to worry about scheduling and completing a sales session. Once you deliver the images, you're done.

- You don't have to offer any product sales if you don't want to, and don't need to buy samples.

- You may choose to still offer sales of prints and other products through your online galleries.

Cons:

- The total income potential for any session is more limited. You need to price your services so that you aren't depending on post-session sales of products.

- There might be greater sales tax liabilities. With IPS, the session fee may be non-taxable, while the delivery of any digital files might be taxed (consult your state for their specific rules). But with an all-inclusive model, it might mean the entire session fee taxable. Research sales tax requirements for your state to determine what is taxable for both sales methods.

- Clients may get overwhelmed by having to choose and purchase prints on their own, and may not end up printing anything.

There is no "correct" answer to how to handle your sales. You may want to try both and see what works best for you. Feedback from your clients can help you understand what's working and what isn't.

How to Know if Your Price is Too Low or Too High

If you're booking every single job you try for, your price is too low. The easiest way to tell that you're underpriced is if you never or rarely hear the word "no." It's not your goal to get every job, it's your goal to create a business that's sustainable long term. If you're doing every job out there, you are likely to get overworked and overwhelmed quickly, and still not be making that much.

If you're not booking much or anything, your price might be too high for your market or skill level. If you really don't want to reduce your price, consider adding other incentives, so you're giving an effective discount. People love free stuff, so maybe instead of dropping your price, you throw in extra photography time for the same price, or prints, or an album. Offering discounts or bonuses, especially limited-time offers, are a great marketing tool to get new business without the appearance of lowering your price.

Retainers and Payment Terms

There are many ways to structure payments for your shoots. A standard practice is to require a retainer at the time of booking and the balance before or at the event.

Retainer v. Deposit: I'm not a lawyer, but I know there is a big difference between the word retainer and the word deposit. While this varies by state, in general, a retainer is an amount paid to reserve services. Because retainers serve a purpose to reserve a time on the calendar, they are normally non-refundable, and usually the amount is applied toward the final balance. On the other hand, a deposit typically gets returned, such as a security deposit for an apartment that gets returned when you move out. So get in the habit of saying "retainer," not "deposit" both in your conversations and your contracts.

Do I need a retainer? Maybe, maybe not. In the very beginning when you're not booked very much, it may not matter if you have a retainer for a date. You just put a shoot on your calendar, and if the client has to cancel, it might not hurt you much. But once your schedule fills up, that time on your calendar is worth money. If a shoot is booked for a prime Saturday afternoon and canceled at the last minute, you miss out on the income from another person who could have filled that time.

In the beginning, I didn't require retainers for portrait sessions. I had one client who would call and book a session or an event, and then she'd cancel every time. She had no respect for my time whatsoever, and I was losing out on real business for the time I held in my calendar for her. As soon as I started requiring retainers to hold the date, she disappeared. She wasn't serious enough about booking anything to put money down. Retainers ensure people are serious about doing the shoot with you.

Fixed or Variable retainers: You can either make your retainers a fixed amount or a percent of the total. I charge a fixed retainer because I don't want to obligate people to pay more up front just because they've booked a bigger package. My retainers are a small, fixed amount (about 25% of a standard booking), which means when I'm shooting more, I have more money. A lot of photographers choose to charge a variable retainer, with 30-50% of the total booked package due up front. This means that when you book a larger package, you'll also make more up front. If you're doing weddings, it's a good way to even out your cash flow, so you're making more in the off-season when you're booking more but shooting less.

Payment Plans: The great thing about a lot of CRMs (Customer Relationship Management) and payment processors is that they allow you to create automated payment plans. You might choose to break down larger payments into monthly or quarterly payments, doing even more to spread out your cash flow.

How you structure your payments is entirely up to you. Over time, you will find out what works best for your business and your cash flow. Just be sure you explain the payment structure clearly so your clients know up front what's expected of them.

When to Require Payment

I suggest requiring payment in full before the shoot begins. My CRM sends out automated emails gently reminding people when their invoice is due.

Many photographers include a contract clause that says they have the right to not show if the client doesn't pay before the event. Personally, I'm a little more forgiving with payment terms, and I allow some people to pay their balance after the event. However, I never provide images, or even begin work on editing them, before I'm paid.

As a friend of mine used to say, "No money now is the first step toward no money ever."

As photographers, we have the advantage of our product being something people really want. It is highly unlikely that someone would have us come out to take photographs, and then just not pay and never get those images. So it is rare for a client not to pay at all, because they know they won't be able to see their images until they do.

If you decide to provide images before you get paid, I can almost guarantee at some point you'll get stiffed. And it might even be from who you would least expect. I've granted leeway to some people in the events industry, people/companies with excellent reputations. I assumed they were good for it, and that leeway bit me in the ass. No matter how much you think you can trust someone, providing images before you get paid is a just a step toward working for free.

It's ok to walk away from a potential client who absolutely refuses to pay before they see the images. Those are usually the same people who will find reasons not to pay you later either, giving empty promises like, "Oh yeah, I'm about to make the payment" before ghosting you entirely. And don't let any client bully you by saying, "But all the other photographers do it the other way." They don't. And if they want to work with you, the only policy that matters is yours.

Just a reminder here that whatever rules you come up with, you have the latitude to extend grace to people when you want to, If you feel like it's the right thing to do. I remember one couple who overextended themselves with the cost of their wedding. They weren't able to pay their balance before the wedding. I said I would still shoot the wedding, but told them I would not even begin editing until they paid in full. They made a few payments when they could, reducing the balance little by little and finally paid the balance after they got a tax refund. I edited and delivered the images two weeks later, almost a year after their wedding. They were a sweet couple who had just gotten into a bad situation, and I felt satisfied that I had made the right decision.

How to Get Paid

There are many ways to exchange money now, including cash, checks, credit cards, ACH transfers, Zelle, CashApp, Venmo, and PayPal. You can really use any of them. I find it most professional to accept payment through multiple methods, so that your customer can use the method that is best for them. That includes taking credit cards directly.

I strongly suggest that once you decide to go professional as a photographer, you sign up for a credit card processor so that you can take credit cards. There are many ways to do it. QuickBooks will allow you to sign up to take credit card payments. HoneyBook (as well as other CRMs) does their own payment processing so it can integrate with your contract & CRM system, or you can sign up for Stripe or other payment processors to take credit cards directly.

For most payment systems, if you are billing clients, you can expect to pay a processing fee, usually just under 3% of the payment total. You have the option of adding that cost to your invoice as a processing fee in most states, but the rules do vary, so you'll need to check local regulations to see if that's legal in your area. Personally, as a consumer I find it really annoying to pay additional fees, so as a business owner I choose to build it in to the price I charge my clients. That just means adding 3% to what you thought your price would be, so that you can cover the costs of processing those payments. I find that to be a much more client-friendly way to do it, so the price you quote will match their invoice.

Believe Your Price

Whatever prices you set, you need to *believe* you're worth it. This is something I struggled with early in my career. When someone asked about price, my answer sounded more like a question than an answer, as if I was apologizing for my price. If you come up with a price and you can't say it out loud without your palms sweating, your eyebrows raising into an apology and your mouth turning into a grimace, you might not be ready for that price point. If you don't believe you're worth it, nobody else will either. You need to communicate your price confidently and know that you are absolutely, positively worth it. If you're not there yet, practice. Say it out loud. It might just be that after hearing it a few (or a few hundred) times, it will become natural to you.

Remember, every photographer's journey is unique. Create a pricing approach that works for you, regardless of what "experts" say you should do, even me. When you create a business, you're carving out your own place in the world and making your own rules.

Chapter 8

Marketing and Promotion

Okay, you have done the hard work to get legal, conducted your research, set your prices, and you have a few jobs under your belt. Now what? How do you help clients to find you and show them you're the right choice?

What is My "Brand?"

We're going to talk a lot about your "brand" in this chapter, so first we should be clear on what that is. Your brand is what defines your services and products. It's your distinct identity. Your brand will include basic things like your company name and logo and design elements, including colors, graphic design, and fonts. It will also include your "voice," meaning how you communicate with clients and potential clients. Is your "voice" professional? Friendly? Casual? Your brand also includes your company's values and mission.

When you're defining your brand, it helps to start with creating a mission. What is your purpose? What values guide you? What kind of experience do you want your customers to have? How do you want your customers to feel when they interact with you? What's your brand's style and voice?

Your answers to all these questions create a picture of your brand that will guide everything you create in your business.

Who Are you Selling To? Defining Your Ideal Client

Before you can develop a marketing strategy, you need to know who you're trying to reach.

Your ideal client appreciates your unique style and artistry. They get along with you as a person. They're willing and able to pay what you're asking.

It helps to create an avatar: an image of the perfect client for your business. How old are they? What's their gender identification? If they showed up at a shoot and were dressed in a way that you loved, what would that be? Bohemian? Elegant? Trendy? What brands are they wearing? Where would they shop? What do they watch on TV? What is their level of education? Do they have children? How about pets? Are they adventurous? Are they eco-conscious?

In the beginning, it might feel like you're pulling answers out of thin air. But it's still valuable. This avatar gives you a picture of what you're shopping for as a client. Imagine you're walking into a big client warehouse and picking out who you think you're going to gel with best. It doesn't have to be perfect, and your ideal client avatar will change over time.

As you get more client experience, you can look back on how your actual clients compare to what you thought was your ideal. Which clients have been the most enjoyable to work with? Who has raved about your photography? Which clients can't you wait to work with again? Or if you've had unpleasant experiences, consider those, and the opposite of that might be what you're looking for. You might find that the best experiences turned out to be with a completely different demographic than you planned. Try not to not cling too tightly to what you thought your avatar might be and develop your vision to include the actual experiences you've had.

Defining your ideal client might seem silly at first, but it allows you to know how to communicate with them. For example, the visuals and messaging that will appeal to a bohemian makeup artist in her early twenties will be very different from a corporate lawyer in their forties. Knowing your target can help you structure all the parts of your message from the colors and words you use to what products and services you offer.

Building an Effective Online Presence

Key word: effective. Lots of photographers kind of fall backwards into their online presence. You might start posting some work on Instagram. Then maybe creating a Dropbox folder full of images people can look at. That's fine for a hobbyist, but a professional needs a website. Because the photos are only part of the story you're telling potential clients. They want to see pretty pictures, but they also want to learn about YOU. They want to understand your brand, and the style and practices that define you.

We are in a uniquely visual field. It's all about what you see. Don't underestimate the value of a cohesive online strategy that's consistent with your brand. That means social media, a website, and all the interactions with clients, friends and others that are visible to the public. Every interaction you have online becomes part of your business.

Creating a Website:

I'm not going to lie, creating a great website can get time consuming and expensive. But it can also be done reasonably. Lots of the online gallery sites (like Pixieset or Zenfolio), allow you to create a website easily, and without having a ton of technical knowledge. And because they link to your online galleries, maintaining a consistent look throughout your galleries becomes easier.

You can also create your own site on a platform like WordPress or Wix. You might need a little more technical knowledge for this, but there are many designers around at a variety of prices to help you.

A few big considerations when you're deciding what platform to choose:

- Visually pleasing templates. Do the site samples for that provider look pretty and have great functionality?

- Responsive design. Do the images and text look good on both a computer, tablet, and phone?

- Speed. Image-heavy websites are a challenge because they can be slow to load. So look at the provider's sample websites and see if they they load quickly.

- Custom domain names. The minimal investment that it takes to get your own domain name is insignificant compared to the difference it makes to clients. How do you tell your clients you're an amateur without saying you're an amateur? By using yoursite.wix.comor something similar instead of your own domain name.

- Email. If you get your own domain name, make sure you can also get an email address using that domain. It's so much more professional that using an address @gmail.com.

- Support. This is imperative. The provider should have 24/7 support. Check reviews that mention support to see if any red flags pop up on the topic. Murphy's law again … If your site goes down, you'll probably find out about it after hours. I've seen photographers suffer with a site that is down or malfunctioning for days or even weeks because their provider's support is unresponsive. Don't let that be you.

- Cost. There is a wide range of hosting solutions, so find one that fits into your budget. It can be hard to switch providers once you choose one, so don't make cost your only deciding factor.

- Search Engine Optimization. Without easy SEO, your website won't matter because it won't be visible in searches. You'll need to learn at least the basics of SEO, and whatever platform you choose for hosting your website may have specific tools for optimizing your SEO.

What to include in your site:

1. **Your Portfolio.** Curate a gallery of your best work that showcases your unique style and expertise in your specific niche. We'll cover more on this later in the chapter.

2. **Your bio.** It may be uncomfortable to write about yourself, but it's how people learn about you and your qualifications. How long have you been shooting? What do you love about photography? What are your favorite things to shoot? Who makes an ideal client for you? Include some things about you that are just fun, that give people an idea of who you are and create a personal connection, like what's on your current playlist, your favorite movies or books, what you do in your spare time, what you're currently obsessed with. Anything quirky or fun that makes you who you are. One note though: there's a lot of random stuff you can share about yourself, so anything you share here needs to be both true and "on brand" with the image you're trying to portray. Look back at the picture of the ideal customer you created and think about what might be a commonality with that person so they might read your bio and think, *"She loves the Bachelor? I love the Bachelor!"*

3. **Contact information.** Clients should be able to contact you in a variety of ways. The communication methods you prefer might take a back seat to your client's preferences. If you love texting and hate emails, be prepared and happy to send emails sometimes, because you want to make it

easy for someone to contact you in the way they prefer.

4. **Links to your social accounts.** You want to encourage people to follow your most current work. Some photographers even display their Instagram feed as a portfolio on their site, ensuring that their current work is always visible.

5. **Blog.** Before you cringe, hear me out. I know, many photographers don't like to blog, because they don't like to write or they think blogging is passé, instead choosing mediums like TikTok or YouTube or stories. But blogging can really help your site's visibility to potential clients. When you blog about a session or a wedding, you can link to all the vendors and locations included in the shoot, making sure that your images and text have good SEO. That way when potential clients are looking for those locations, vendors, or topics, they'll find you, and hopefully they'll love your images. And showcasing the work of other vendors and your clients is also great for building community. Keep in mind that If you start blogging, you'll need to keep it up. A neglected blog where your last post is from two years ago might be worse than not having one at all, because it might appear like you haven't worked in a while.

Deciding whether to publish your pricing

When you did your market research, you probably found that lots of photographers don't publicly show their pricing. Why?

Some photographers feel they want clients to choose them based on their work, not based on price. By not publishing your pricing, you can emphasize the value and expertise you bring to the table, rather than focusing solely on the price. This approach allows you to have a conversation with potential clients, understand their needs, and demonstrate the unique benefits they will receive by choosing your services. It also requires a little more "selling" of your value proposition to potential clients.

You also might not want to publish your pricing if you plan to charge different prices to different customers. You may want to charge more to corporate clients than you do to individuals, or you might work on events that vary widely in time, effort, and cost. If your deliverables change for each job, custom pricing is the way to go.

There's also a niche of luxury photography that considers published pricing to be in poor taste. The message they're sending is, "If you have to ask, you can't afford it." It appeals to clients who value exclusivity and prestige.

Personally, I publish all my pricing online (mostly). Here's why:

Transparency and trust: When you publish your pricing, it creates transparency and builds trust with potential clients. My clients know exactly what to expect. The only pricing I don't publish is for some events and branding sessions, because they vary too widely in deliverables, time, and effort to have a set price.

Saving time and energy for both you and your client: In the beginning, I listened to others who thought you shouldn't publish pricing. I spent way too much time on calls and emails asking one question: "how much?" Most price shopping calls mean they're looking for the lowest price, which usually isn't me, even back then. I don't want to waste my time with inquiries that won't go anywhere, and I don't want to waste my client's time either. As a consumer, I probably wouldn't look at a photographer who didn't publish their pricing because I wouldn't want to take extra time to go through a sales presentation just to find out I can't afford it. But that's just me. My opinion isn't nearly as important as your target client's opinion.

Curating Your Portfolio

This is one of the hardest things for a photographer to do. How do you decide what to show?

Show the images you *love*. Include the images that make you most proud. The images that made you realize you have something to offer in this field.

Show what you want to do more of. Let's say you're a studio photographer. You have done some outdoor photography and you love the images you've created, but you would prefer to work in your studio. Don't show the outdoor stuff. Only show the work that you want to do more of.

Quality over quantity. You don't need to have hundreds of images in your portfolio. Most people won't look at the entire thing anyway, so choose only your absolute best images.

Organize. Keep images together from each niche. You'll have a gallery for studio portraits, one for weddings, one for headshots, every niche you serve should have its own gallery.

Consider the order. Since most people won't look at an entire portfolio, your strongest images should be at the very beginning. Sometimes a person looks through and as soon as they see an image that really resonates with them, they will decide to contact you.

Get feedback. Show your portfolio to other photographers or to people in your target market and ask them what you should keep and what you should get rid of. But don't ask just anyone. The people you ask should be in or near your target market. If you're targeting brides in their early twenties with a free spirit vibe, don't ask your stuffy uncle Leopold for his opinion. He's probably not going to like the images that would appeal to your target.

Once in a while, you can ignore the portfolio feedback from others. It can be a painful experience when you love an image and people tell you they don't think it belongs in your portfolio. They might say it's not representative of your best work, but you *freakin' love* this image. Sometimes an image just speaks to your soul, and all you want to do is create more like it. Keep it in your portfolio. I had an image like this. No one else loved it but me, but I felt strongly about it and kept it in my portfolio. Then one day I was talking to a potential client and she brought up how much she loved that one image. I melted. I knew right then that she was a perfect client for me, because she *got me.* Sometimes if I create an image like this, I'll put it out on social media or a blog with an explanation of why it's special to me and ask who it resonates with. The answer might be nobody. It can be fun to see when a controversial image appeals to certain people.

Update Regularly. You'll need to update your portfolio at least annually. Forever. But in the beginning, consider adding your new favorite images to your portfolio at least quarterly. As your work grows, you want to continually add your favorite images and remove the ones you've grown away from. A young photography business is like a baby ... they grow and change so quickly and you have to keep up.

Using Social Media for Business

Social media might be the way you first showed your work to people. Comments like "you're so talented!" might be what got you interested in creating a photography business. Even if you're already a social media pro, there are different considerations for using it for your business.

- Be consistent across platforms. Make your work consistent across your website, Instagram, Facebook, Pinterest, YouTube and more. Remove any pre-business images that no longer fit your aesthetic or brand, or start a new feed altogether.

- Learn about your target clients. Social media is a great place to find out about your target market. You can see what they like, what they buy, what matters to them. You can get a great sense of what's appealing to them, because they probably post about it.

- Engage. Don't be a silent scroller. Get out there and engage with vendors and clients. Like and comment on the accounts you want to stay in front of. Social media is one big networking party.

- Find niche interest groups. Use hashtags to search for topics you're interested in, and use those hashtags in your posts to increase your visibility. You can find your people through hashtags. There's an entire art to finding the right hashtags. Social media management tools like Tailwind and others can help you identify the most effective hashtags.

- Collaborate. One of the best ways to grow your reach is collaborating with others. You can work with other vendors in your field to create content that appeals to both of your audiences.

- Track your competitors and role models. Follow other photographers who produce images you strive to create. It'll keep you inspired. Pay attention to what your role models post and the tone of what they write. When you do this, just make sure it's to stay inspired, not to copy.

- Ask for shoots. As you build your portfolio, you can post about what you want to do and ask who is interested. You will get volunteers. But don't "borrow" another photographer's work to show it as an example, even if you say "this is not my photo." This is the easiest way to offend other photographers and create a bad reputation in the field. The only thing you should ever post is your own work.

- Show yourself. People on social media don't just want to see the work you create, they want to learn about you. For people like me who are way more comfortable behind the camera than in front of one, it can be tough to put yourself out there. Try to show some behind the scenes photos or videos and talk about your work a little, or give a glimpse into your personal life.

Separating Your Personal and Business Social Media:

In most cases you should have separate business and personal accounts. That way, your business can show your work and build your brand while you still have a place to talk about your personal life. There's also the question of whether or not you should restrict the viewing of your personal profile. If you like to get into controversial topics or political discussions on your personal page, you should probably restrict viewing of that account to just your close friends. If you wouldn't talk about it in a potential client meeting, it probably shouldn't be public.

If your previous social media has been a little messy, you also might want to consider a service like LifeBrand to clean up anything in your social media past that could affect a client's decision to hire you.

Social Media Management

As you grow, you will need a social media management tool to stay on top of your posts. These tools can help you schedule your posts for the most effective times, be consistent across multiple channels, find hashtags, plan your feed, and even help you write your posts with AI. There are many options, each with their own benefits, including Buffer, Hootsuite, SocialPilot, and Tailwind.

Many of them offer free trials so you can test them out to see which resonates best with you and meets your budget.

Email Marketing

Building an email list is a great way to keep in touch with your clients. You can create newsletters to update your followers about your recent work, upcoming events or mini sessions. Create a reason for people to sign up, such as discounts, bonuses, or being the first to know about new offerings. The frequency of communication is up to you, but it's essential to be respectful of your clients' inboxes. We've all gotten annoyed when we signed up for an email list and then got bombarded with too many messages or emails that repeat useless content. Think about your email communications as if you've been invited into your client's home. Don't be rude and don't overstay your welcome. If you appear in their inbox, you should have a reason, and that reason needs to benefit your client, not you.

The industry standard right now as of this writing is Mailchimp. It gives you the ability to create attractive emails pretty easily, and has features for managing your communications, like seeing how many people opened or read your emails and tracking clicks to your website. This area is growing among CRMs too, and you might find a CRM that has features to help you grow your email list and send newsletters.

Advertising

Sometimes social media and networking aren't enough to get you work. You may want to consider advertising.

Where to Advertise:

- Google business listings. You can list your business with google for free.

- Local business listings. You can promote your business for free or cheap on local listing sites, like Nextdoor, Bing, Yelp, Angi, CitySearch, and more. Creating these links also gives you valuable backlinks to your website, which helps your overall SEO.

- Facebook/Instagram ads. This is a great place to start with advertising, since you can target who sees your ad based on their demographics, like location, income, hobbies, and who they follow.

- LinkedIn. this is great if you're trying to reach other business owners for product and branding shoots, or headshots.

- Vendor directories. In the wedding market there are a ton of options, such as WeddingPro/The Knot, and other wedding magazines.

- Print ads in magazines. Bridal magazines are a straightforward choice if you're shooting weddings. For other specialties, you can find local city or community magazines that offer advertising at reasonable rates.

How do you decide what advertising opportunities fit your business? Here are some things to consider when you're evaluating them:

1. Is my target market going to see this?

2. What is my goal? How will I know if this ad is successful? Is it visits to my website, how many shoots I've booked, or just name recognition in my area?

3. Do I have a unique message that will draw people in?

What to Include In Your Ad:

- A compelling image (or images) that perfectly showcases your style and will appeal to your target client.

- Your website and contact information.

- A reason for them to contact you, such as a special promotion. These can be great seasonal options, like promoting new headshots at the beginning of a new year, or family photos for Christmas cards.

- A call to action. There should be a clear next step in your ad, like "book your session now" or "learn more"

There are entire books written on advertising strategy, so before you take the leap I recommend doing some research into what's successful in your niche. Since the cost involved in advertising can be significant, the best place to start is by clearly defining your goals and strategy.

Incentives: Bonuses and Discounts

Incentives can persuade people who were just considering hiring you to take action. You can either offer promotional prices for a limited time, or as a part of your overall package creation. The difference between them is discounts reduce the price your client pays, while bonuses offer something extra for paying the full price. There are benefits and disadvantages to both.

Discounts: Discounts are probably the most popular promotion tool for any kind of product or service. When your business is new, discounts allow you to set your desired market price while still incentivizing clients to hire you while the price is still low. It sends a clear message that the low price is temporary. Some photographers don't love offering discounts because they think they appeal to price shoppers, which can be true. If you offer discounts, you'll want to use a few best practices.

- Make the discount significant. It needs to be a big enough discount to make a difference, whether it be in a dollar amount or a percent. 10-20% or more is a good starting place.

- Give a reason for the discount. We're all used to seeing sales for a purpose, like holiday sales. You can also use events like your birthday, the anniversary of your business, or other fun days.

- Make it a limited time offer. Discounts are typically more effective if they have an expiration date. Give people a reason to act within a limited time.

- Don't inflate the original price in order to offer the discount. When you do this, it erodes your client's trust, and they might feel like they're getting scammed.

Bonuses: Instead of discounts, you can choose to offer items for free or at a reduced price when your customer makes a purchase. For instance, I give away an engagement session for free with any wedding booking. You can offer bonuses for a limited time, or they can be a part of your regular offering. You can offer service bonuses, like extra session time, or free album design, or you can give away products, like free or discounted prints. Bonuses are great for getting clients to level up to bigger packages. If you offer three packages, you could skip the bonus in the basic package, offer a small bonus in the middle package (such as album upgrades) and a big bonus in your top package (such as a print credit or free album copies).

Networking

Local networking is a great way to meet people and find new business. There are industry groups for the wedding and events industry, like WIPA (the Wedding International Professionals Association). When you join the Chamber of Commerce or similar groups you will meet other business owners in your area. You can also find meetup groups online that offer the chance to meet people in your target market.

Getting Published

Getting your work published in magazines and blogs is a great way to get in front of new potential clients and vendors. This is big in the wedding industry, but also good for other types of editorial and family photographers. Online and print magazines are always looking for real content to inspire their readers, and all you need to do is submit your work to them.

Don't just submit your work blindly. Pay attention to the style and content in the magazine or blog you're submitting to. If they always post dark and moody images and yours are full color, you're wasting your time and theirs. If you have a shoot that you think is worthy of publication, make sure it matches the style you're already seeing in that magazine. The cute DIY backyard wedding you just shot will not be a good fit for Grace Ormand, no matter how beautifully it is photographed.

If getting your work published is something you aspire to, you'll need to shoot with that goal in mind. Look at what gets published in the magazines you want to be in. Is it fashion focused? Are they looking for unique details? Whatever those things are, you can adjust your shot list to ensure you capture the type of images that get published.

Two Bright Lights is a great online source for finding where your work might get published and creating submissions to editors. Editors will even put out requests for certain types of content they're looking for.

Remember to get written permission from your clients before you submit any photos of them for publication. If they don't agree to the publication, you will embarrass yourself and hurt your future chances with a magazine if they prepare an article only to find their time was wasted because the client did not consent.

Don't Steal Other Artists' Work!

I mentioned this before, but it happens so often in the industry that it bears repeating and elaborating.

As a photographer, your work is your art, your passion, and your livelihood. Just as you expect others to respect and value your creative efforts, it is equally imperative to extend the same courtesy to fellow photographers. Stealing, or as some say, "borrowing" photos, not only violates copyright laws but also undermines the integrity and professionalism of the entire photography community.

Here's a scenario: You see someone's milk bath photos, and you want to do a shoot with a milk bath. So you post some photos saying "who wants to do this?" Along with some photos "borrowed" from the original photographer, for "inspiration." You don't think you've done anything wrong, but in reality, this little activity is called copyright infringement and could result in public embarrassment, damage to your reputation, and fines of up to thousands of dollars.

Not only is this not a gray area legally, it is also considered highly unethical. There is at least one entire website dedicated to exposing and making an example of people who steal other photographer's work. It can literally ruin your career. So the bottom line is, never use another photographer's work unless you have express written permission from them to do so.

What about stock photography? Can you purchase a stock photo to show on your social media or website? No. When you show work that isn't yours, you decrease the trust level between you and your clients. All of a sudden, they can't be sure if what they're seeing is your work or not. I've seen stories of photographers getting sued by clients because they used stock photos in their portfolio and then couldn't deliver results consistent with those images. Whether or not you think you can deliver the results, showing someone else's work, even if you've purchased it, is misleading at best.

Stealing doesn't just apply to photos. Don't steal music either. If you even create a slideshow to music, you could be breaking copyright laws and subjecting yourself to fines. If you use music, you must properly license it.

Also, watch out for copyrighted or trademarked characters. Every year I see photographers promoting mini sessions that include the Grinch character, or other characters. Do not do this! You can't use material created by someone else in order to sell your own services. Those characters are owned by companies that have every right to come after you and take legal action. I've seen it happen many, many times, and it simply isn't worth it.

Remember, creating and maintaining a successful photography business is not just about taking beautiful photographs. It's about conducting yourself with integrity, respecting the work of others, and maintaining an excellent reputation within the industry.

Chapter 9

Making Each Photoshoot a Success

Now let's walk through the day-to-day in this business. How do you make every shoot a success?

Getting your mind right

I believe this to be true:

> *What differentiates an average photo from an exceptional one is what is in the heart and mind of the photographer when they click the shutter.*

It's why two photographers can be in the same place at the same time and produce completely different results. There is a reason Ansel Adams' photos stand out from the multitude of other landscapes. Sure, it's because of his patience in waiting for the right moment, but it's also because what comes through in his photography is a loving awe of the beauty of nature. It helps to not just see, but to celebrate your subject.

What you are thinking and feeling when you're shooting will come through in the final product, much like how you can practically taste the love in a thoughtfully prepared meal. If you go to a shoot in a bad mood or are just phoning it in, that will show up in the photos. So if you're having a bad day, find a way to turn it around before you start shooting. Take deep breaths, center yourself, and focus on making the shoot the best possible experience for your client. Decide to make their day.

Preparing for the Shoot

Try not to walk into any photoshoot not knowing what to expect. Gather information about how many people will be involved, their relationship to each other, any interpersonal issues or physical limitations. Create a shot list if you need one. If you're shooting on site, you may find it helpful to take a field trip ahead of time to the site so you can see what you have to work with and plan out shots and angles if need be.

Especially in the beginning, if you have nerves going into new shoots, preparation can really help to ease your mind.

Organizing Your Gear

Before every shoot, get your gear organized and ready. Do these things before every shoot:

- The day/night before, charge your batteries and spare

batteries.

- Make sure you have room on the memory cards you'll be using. I suggest formatting the cards before a session so you have a blank slate to work with. Bring extra cards just in case you fill up the primary or something happens to the card.

- Before every shoot, make a checklist of everything you need to bring, including cameras, lighting, light modifiers, stands, cards, batteries, and other supplies like props, lens wipes, hand sanitizer, tissues or snacks.

- If need be, clean your lenses before the shoot.

The Importance of Being Early

I always joke that in Atlanta, there is no such thing as on time. You're either late or early to everything, because traffic can vary so widely. Going across town might take 15 minutes, or it might take an hour.

When you're dealing with clients, you need to be on time. Always. Clients need to know that when they're paying for your time, they get what they pay for. It's incredibly disrespectful of your client's time to be late. If you live in a place with unpredictable traffic, plan to be early to avoid even the chance of being late. It is a central practice of professionalism.

Be ready to shoot at the session time. If you have a shoot scheduled for 5 pm, that means you should be able to make the first click of the shutter at 5 pm, not be pulling in to the parking lot at 5 pm. Figure out how much time you need to set up, and be early by that amount of time so that you can be fully set and ready to go the moment the session time starts.

If you have to be late through some circumstance outside your control, communicate. Let your client know the minute you know. Thank them for their patience, and if they get inconvenienced, offer something special to make up for it. A gift card to their favorite coffee shop is a nice touch, or you can add free products to their photography package. Whatever you choose, it will go a long way to show them that their business matters to you.

Posing and Directing Clients

If you're uncomfortable with posing, know you're not alone. I was too. I wasn't confident about posing, and I didn't like the artificial poses that I saw in so many photos. Luckily posing is an area of photography with almost unlimited resources, including books, cheat sheets, videos, and classes.

How you pose clients becomes part of your photography style, and ultimately your brand.

Consider the images you want to create. How are the subjects posed? Is it formal or casual? Do they look "posed" or do they look candid? Just because a photo captures a real moment doesn't mean it's not posed. It's all about the magic you create once your subject gets into position.

Whatever your style of posed or candid photos, you will get the best results if you help your clients feel comfortable and relaxed. Provide clear direction, but be gentle in your instructions. Always direct them toward a better pose rather than make them feel they're doing it wrong. Be open to their ideas and suggestions. If you sense they are uncomfortable in any pose, keep adjusting until it works.

Not all poses work for all people. Even if you develop a go-to list of poses, they won't work on everyone. What works depends on a person's personality, physical needs, and things you probably can't even account for, like how they feel about their looks, or if they have a "good side." Even if a particular pose works for you 99% of the time, if it doesn't work for someone, don't force it. Just move on to the next thing.

As you pose subjects during your session, don't touch anyone physically without their permission. I've seen lots of photographers charge toward their clients to move an arm or fix a stray hair, only to see the client flinch with discomfort. Before you touch anyone, just ask, "Are you ok with me moving this stray hair out of place?"

Overtime

Sometimes you'll find yourself at the end of your scheduled shoot time and you haven't gotten what you needed from the shoot. Maybe someone was late, or you've had to deal with an uncooperative child. How should you handle it? My approach depends a lot on the client's situation. Sometimes running late is no one's fault, and I'll be happy to go overtime a little, assuming we're able to in that location. I try not to be a stickler for time if it's not significant. I would rather run a little late (10-15 minutes) at no charge than to have the client feel like I'm nickel-and-diming them.

But sometimes I can tell that a client is just trying to get more than they paid for, and I'll be a little less flexible, letting them know that I'm happy to stay longer for $x if they want to extend their time.

There also will be times that you just don't have the option to go late, because you're in a rented studio, or because you have another session immediately after. I always try to check in with the client 5-10 minutes before the session is over, saying that we are running out of time and giving them the option to prioritize how we spend our last minutes. That way they can get what they need before the time runs out and they're not taken by surprise by having to end abruptly.

Protecting of Your Gear And Images

I've seen horror stories through the years of how careless storage of gear resulted in tragedy.

Never leave your gear unattended in your car with images you just shot. I've too many stories about how a photographer went to a shoot, left their gear in the car overnight, and returned to find it had all been stolen, including the images. Your camera gear is your livelihood. Never leave it overnight in your car.

Particularly for weddings, if I absolutely need to stop somewhere on the way home, I take the cards out of the camera and keep them in a secure in a bag or pocket on my body. If my car should get broken into, I might lose my gear, but I won't lose an entire wedding's images.

Post-Production and Deliverables

You're not done when the client walks out the door. Now you need to deliver the images by the promised time, at a quality consistent with what you've delivered in the past.

When a client sees your portfolio, they expect the result they get will match what they see. Before you deliver images, ask yourself if the quality is as good or better than what you've delivered in the past. If not, go back and continue working with them until you can feel proud and want to show them off. Consistency is key.

Chapter 10

Delivering Exceptional Client Experience

The client experience includes every single touchpoint from the first time they hear about you to well after their session is over. Every ad, social media post, meeting, chat, photoshoot, and framed photo. So when you think about the client experience, don't just think about the day of the shoot. It's an entire lifetime of interactions.

Client Interactions

Photography is personal. We spend a lot of time with our clients. On a wedding day, we might spend more time with each member of the couple than they spend with each other.

The most fundamental part of customer service is listening to your clients. Take time to understand what they want to get out of their shoot, how they'll use their photos, and any special meaning the photos have in their life or their business.

I always say I fall a little in love with every one of my clients. I want to learn about them and focus on their positive qualities. I want to know what makes them laugh. I want to know if they want to feel like a supermodel during their session, or if they are uncomfortable in front of the camera and need some hand holding. No matter what kind of photography you're doing, try to bring out the beauty of the subject, whether it's a person, a product, or a pet. Don't just look at them, celebrate them. That energy will come across to your clients and in their photos.

The Extra Mile

Going above and beyond expectations is what truly sets your service apart from the crowd. It's what transforms a client who is happy with your service to one who wants to shout your name from the rooftops. Surprise your clients with small gestures that show you value them, whether it's a thank-you note, a personalized gift, or offering an additional service at no cost. I send custom thank-you cards featuring my logo with final wedding deliverables like albums or USB drives. I've also experimented with different thank you gifts, like finding out a couple's favorite wedding photo and gifting them a free framed print. If you sell products, create pretty packaging so they're beautifully presented. If you don't have the budget to invest in gifts for your clients, a simple thank you goes a long way to let them know you appreciate their business. Any acts of kindness will leave a lasting impression and make your clients feel appreciated.

Establishing Long-Term Relationships

I'm a big fan of creating friendships with my clients. I'll friend them on social media so I can connect with them before or between sessions. I love seeing what's happening in their lives. I buy Girl Scout cookies from their kids. I wish them a happy birthday. It's important though, to be genuine in these interactions. I'm not doing it to get more business, I'm doing it because I actually care. Don't think your clients won't be able to tell the difference.

Mistakes and Challenges: What to Do When Things Go Wrong

Be prepared for this: Things will go wrong in your business. No matter how hard you try, it will happen. You might have a shoot that doesn't go well, experience an unhappy client, make a mistake, or forget to respond to someone. It's not the end of the world, but the mistake itself is often less memorable than how you handle it.

Problems usually fall into a couple of areas:

- Miscommunication. A client may not understand the costs involved, or maybe there's a misunderstanding about what was supposed to happen during a session, or what or when you would be delivering images.

- Technical challenges. Equipment malfunctions, corrupted cards, car trouble, any technical failure that means you're late, or unable to perform a shoot or deliver images.

- Sickness. At some point you will get sick and not be able to do a shoot.

When something bad happens, it's all about how you deal with it.

Be proactive. No matter what the problem is, address it head on. Communicate with your client about what the problem is, and be ready to offer solutions, whether it be a re-shoot, a free session or some other consolation.

Listen. If your client approaches you with a concern, listen thoughtfully. Avoid making excuses and instead put your energy into making your client feel heard, understood, and valued.

Be contrite. I see so many photographers deal with conflict poorly. They get indignant and argumentative. They think they're right and want the client to know it. This approach makes it more likely that your client will not come back to you again, and they may even give you a critical review or tell their friends about their awful experience.

Don't rely on your contract to solve issues. Relying on your contract in the face of a potential conflict with a client is a last resort. Yes, your contract is there to spell out terms and conditions and remedies, but if you have to rely on your contract in the face of potential legal actions, the situation has already gotten out of control. Try to resolve the situation before it comes to legal action.

There is a tendency among photographers to add terms to their contract every time something bad happens. They don't get fed a meal at one wedding, so they build it into the contract that they must get a hot meal. A guest at a wedding is obnoxious, so they add in terms about being able to leave if they feel offended by a guest. Soon their contract is a five-page bloated mess of terms involving scenarios that don't happen very often, which can make the client feel suspicious or intimidated by all the rules and regulations. I'm not going to say you can't add every possible scenario into your contract, I'm just suggesting that it makes a statement about your business when you do. You'll maintain better relationships with your clients if your go-to move in difficult times is communication and a goal of mutually beneficial resolution rather than metaphorically smacking someone on the nose with a rolled up contract.

Google it! If you're not good at communicating under pressure, you can buy pre-written emails for dealing with difficult situations. Whatever the situation you find yourself in, someone has probably been there before, and there are lots of resources to help you communicate effectively, even if it doesn't come naturally to you.

Chapter 11
Special Considerations for Weddings

The wedding industry isn't for everyone. In fact, I think it's the type of photography that will most quickly burn people out. It's a long, physically demanding day. You'll be carrying lots of equipment and walking miles before the day is over. You will deal with all kinds of personalities and family dynamics. There's stress up the wazoo. You might encounter bridezillas and groomzillas and momzillas. But you'll also share the happiest days of your clients' lives. You'll see beautiful decor and share in loving moments. You'll hear great bands. You'll laugh. You'll eat cake.

Honing Your Wedding Skills

- **Awareness.** Be constantly watching and listening for what's going on around you. Glasses clinking, laughter, dancing. You'll be using all your senses all day to be in a heightened state of awareness.

- **Quick Response.** As I'm watching for activity during the day, I try to keep my camera at or near my face. Things happen quickly, and you may only have a second or two to see what's happening, frame it up, and click the shutter. If your camera is at your side, or even worse, not in your hands at all, you're likely to miss out on valuable moments even when you see them, because you just can't make it happen quickly enough.

- **Anticipation.** If you wait for a moment to happen, it will be over before you can take the photo. Watch for someone who is telling a funny story, and be ready for the punchline and laughter that results. Watch the bar for shots being poured so you can get the clink of glasses. Watch as people approach each other from across a room, so you can capture a heartfelt hug and the smiles as they greet each other.

- **Planning.** Do all your planning well in advance of the wedding. I try to gather everything I need to know, including a shot list, locations, timeline, and names of important people at least two weeks before the wedding. There is a lot of stress right before a wedding, so I try not to bother the couple with any questions in the week or two before the wedding date. And for the love of God, don't ask logistical questions of the bride on the wedding day. It just adds to her stress. Getting a shot list ahead of time is a must, since on the wedding day it's much more likely that something will get forgotten. There's just too much other activity going on to remember everything.

- **Preparation**. If you only have a few minutes for portraits, don't wait until the start of that time to have your lights set up. Get set and ready and do some test shots so that when your client is ready, you can be shooting immediately. A few minutes before any event (like cake cutting, first dance, bouquet toss, etc.), I go to the spot where I'll be shooting and do some test shots to check lighting and framing before the client gets into place. Don't take the chance of missing key moments or delaying the action because you're not set up.

- **Time Management.** If you've done good planning for a wedding, you know exactly how much time you have to shoot specific things. Nothing annoys clients and other vendors more (which will affect your referrals) than a photographer ignoring their schedule. If the schedule is running late because of someone else, if you can make up some time, you'll be a hero.

- **Consistency.** The fun (and sometimes scary) thing about weddings is that you'll encounter a vast array of circumstances. The challenge is to produce consistent results. Strive with every wedding to create images that are portfolio-worthy. And that means consistency regardless of the venue. It doesn't matter if you're in a beautiful ballroom or a back alley, that client deserves quality images. You just might have to be a little more creative to make some settings look more appealing.

- **Constant improvement.** Consistency is the first step, but even beyond that, strive to make every wedding your best one ever.

- **Interest.** There is no reason to be bored at a wedding. I know plenty of photographers who will zone out during the reception. Yes, I've been at weddings where there are four hours of the same people dancing, and I think, "I can't possibly take any more photos of these people that are going to look any different." Instead of standing around looking bored, embrace the opportunity to try something new. Try lighting the dance floor a different way, or using a lens you rarely use during the reception. Look for the details around the room that tell a story, like the candles that have burned down or the crumbs on the cake plate. The moments where you could get bored are the best times to grow in your skills and increase your awareness of the elements of storytelling.

- **Communication.** There are so many variables at a wedding, and anything can change at any moment. You'll want to cultivate open, friendly communication with the planner/coordinator, and the DJ or band. Those are the people who make things happen during the day, so being on the same page with them will help avoid surprises. Check in with them often.

- **Attention to Detail.** Be watching for the little details that will make a difference. The most obvious is making sure the bride's gown is laying perfectly, but small details abound. Is the groom's bow tie crooked? Can you see everyone's faces in a group photo? This area is something you'll learn from experience. It's often after something gets missed that you start to watch for it in the future. Once you have to re-take an entire set of wedding party photos because you didn't notice the groomsmen didn't have their boutonnieres on, you probably won't forget it again.

- **Helpfulness.** I approach every wedding with an attitude of service. "Seva" is a Sanskrit word meaning "selfless service" or "dedication to others," and it's the attitude of joyfully serving. Sure, the clients are paying me, but I consider the entire day to be an act of love toward my clients and their guests. I try to be helpful throughout the day, whether it be pinning on a boutonniere, bringing emergency kit items like extra safety pins or wet wipes. I can't tell you how many times I've seen someone upset over a stain on their dress or suit and been able to pull out the stain remover. It makes me happy every time I can help someone out. I have a mini emergency kit with safety pins, sewing supplies, fashion tape, scissors, nail clippers, stain remover, hand sanitizer, and more with me at the wedding, so I'm ready for anything.

- **Personal service.** Call people by name as much as possible. A wedding day is a very personal thing for people, and no one wants to be called "bride" or "groom." Know the names of all the important people so you can address them personally, not by their role. I try to know the names of the bride and groom, their parents and siblings, and as much of the wedding party as my memory will allow. Sometimes if the wedding party is huge, I won't be able to learn all their names, but I'll at least know the Maid/Matron of Honor and Best Man. This will make your job easier, too, because if you need to adjust people in a group photo, you'll be able to say "Linda, can you move a little to the left?" Instead of "Hey, you with the dark hair ..." I'm not great with names either, so I keep the list handy at all times so I can remember.

- **Problem solving.** Things will go wrong. Plan on it. In fact, it is pretty rare for everything to go as planned on a wedding day. It might be rain at an outdoor wedding, a wardrobe malfunction, people being late, or equipment malfunction. When something comes up, don't just complain about it. It's your time to jump in and think of ways to adjust. I have often helped brainstorm ways to adjust the schedule when the couple ran late, bustled wedding gowns, fixed someone's hair, safety-pinned a dress, and even given the bride and groom a ride when their limo didn't show.

- **Flexibility.** I go into every wedding with a plan. And I also end up abandoning those plans more often than not because something changes. I usually arrive early at a venue so I can plan out where I'll do certain shots, only for the light to change in that spot by the time everyone is ready. For every plan, have a plan B. Having an attitude of going with the flow will really help lower your stress levels. I used to get really stressed when things weren't going as planned. Eventually, being flexible with changing plans started to feel good. It can feel really empowering to turn something going wrong into something great. When you realize that adjusting to events as they change is actually a skill, you can turn flexibility into your own superpower.

Rate yourself on these items after every wedding. You might find that you do really well in some areas and not as well in others. Then you know how to adjust your approach for the next wedding.

Don't be:

- Stubborn. Yes, you ran late because of the hair and makeup artist, but that doesn't mean you should dig in your heels and force the rest of the day to run late. Do what you can to help with problems, even if they're not your fault. Everyone at the wedding needs to work together to give the clients the best possible experience. Your positive attitude will pay off in referrals and happy clients.

- Lazy. People pay a lot for wedding photography, and it's a momentous day in their life. They don't want to see someone standing around looking bored. Find things to shoot even if you think you've done it all.

- Unengaged. People also don't want to see you on your phone, texting or making calls. Put the phone away and keep it on silent. The only people you should talk to via text or phone during the day are your team of vendors, in order to communicate what's happening and timelines. If you absolutely must take a call or text because of an emergency, remove yourself to outside or the bathroom so you're not seen by your clients and their guests.

- Critical. I have a rule to never speak disparagingly about anything or anyone at a wedding. Don't criticize what someone's wearing, the details or decor, or even someone's nasty attitude. You never know when someone might overhear, and that's not a good look. You don't want your snarky comments getting back to your client. After the event is over, go home and bitch to your co-workers or friends or significant other, but don't say anything negative while you are at an event.

Building a Referral Network

The more you become familiar with the wedding industry, you'll find vendors you admire and want to work with. You might see their work in magazines or in social media and think, "Wow, I really want to work with them." In your excitement, you might think you can approach them and show them your work and they will want to work with you. But it's not that easy. Especially in the wedding industry, there's so much more to it than your portfolio. Before vendors will work with you, they want to know that not only can you create images, but you're dependable, easy to work with, and follow through with giving them images. I hear so many vendors say their biggest complaint about photographers is that they can't get images from them. The simple gesture of providing images to your vendor friends ("Friendors") will go a long way to getting you referrals. Providing your images to vendors also will expand your reach, since you'll be visible to everyone shopping for other services like florals, venues, caterers, and favors.

If you want to get great vendor referrals, make a practice of capturing beautiful photos of their items from the wedding day. The photos of a vendor's products need to be good enough for them to post on anything from social media to ads to delivery vans. My goal at every wedding is to capture magazine-worthy images of everything down to the smallest detail: custom napkins, favors, or the engraved knife for cutting the cake. I try to make each one of those elements look beautiful, as if each vendor had hired me to get images of it. I do this for two reasons:

1. Wedding planning is incredibly time-intensive and expensive. Couples put a ton of energy into every detail, only to have the day go by so fast they can't appreciate it. I've captured photos of many details only to have the couple tell me later that they are grateful for the photos because they never got to see it on the actual wedding day.

2. Providing those images to vendors helps everyone. If vendors want to show off your images, you'll get greater reach into their following. Plus, they'll want to refer people to you, because when they do, they know they'll get more gorgeous images.

You don't have to provide photos to vendors for free. Many photographers choose to charge vendors for the right to use their photos, and that price may differ whether it's on social media or ads. That's fine. The copyright remains with you, the photographer, and you can set whatever rules you like. For my business, I don't charge vendors for photos unless I'm doing a shoot specifically for them. I approach this with the goal of creating community and helping my fellow small business owners, and that has resulted in a wonderful community of vendors who share referrals.

Doing Styled Shoots

In the beginning of your career, you might not have a lot to show. How do you show work if you're not working a lot yet? You might consider collaborating with wedding planners, florists, makeup artists, and other vendors to create your own styled shoot. These shoots can be beneficial for everyone because the vendors get to be creative and they get photos of their work, and you get experience shooting the things you want to shoot. I did lots of styled shoots early in my career, and I created friendships with vendors that have lasted many years because of it.

There are also companies that will charge for you to participate in styled shoots. They often hire luxury vendors to create a styled set and hire models, and then many photographers participate, shooting their own version of the scene. I don't recommend these, since they can be expensive and you might end up having images that other photographers in your area are showing very similar versions of. It's probably better for you to reach out to vendors you know to create your own vision.

Chapter 12

Growing Your Business

You're off to a great start. You built a solid foundation and now you're looking for how to grow sustainably, all while improving your processes. What kinds of things will help take your business to the next level?

Getting Referrals and Reviews

Word-of-mouth referrals are more valuable than ever. For most photographers, after a few years in business, referrals will become the primary source of business. When your clients are happy, they will post their photos and their friends will ask, "Who did your photos?" People are much more likely to buy a product or service if they personally know someone who has had an enjoyable experience, especially with something as personal as photography.

To encourage referrals, consider implementing a referral program or offering incentives for clients who refer new customers. This not only rewards your existing clients, it also helps to expand your client base. You can reward referrals with small gifts, thank-you notes, or bonuses for future sessions. I once offered a client a discount for every additional client she referred, and we ended up booking an entire day of sessions in her neighborhood. Her session ended up being free, and I was thrilled to give it to her.

I send a questionnaire after every wedding asking the clients to rate me as if they're doing a review online. When I get a 5 star review back, I'll ask them to share it with the world and provide links, making it as easy as possible for them. If you have a CRM you can automate this process, sending questionnaires after each shoot and referring happy clients to where they can post them online.

You can also take quotes from those questionnaires and reviews and post them on your social media, website, and all your marketing channels. Show off your happy customers everywhere!

Outsourcing and Automation

In the beginning, you may be able to tackle every task by yourself, but as you grow, that becomes more complicated. It may also be a challenge to keep up with tasks while this is a side hustle. After all, you might have an entire day job to work around, plus the needs of your relationship or family. Starting and running business is very time consuming.

We talked about CRMs in Chapter 4, and I suggest getting started with one sooner rather than later. It's so common to get overwhelmed in this business and you might not see it coming until you're under water. Automating repetitive tasks and having a central location for all your business information is a fundamental step toward making your business sustainable long term.

You can also outsource when time gets tight. There are people out there just waiting to take over photography tasks like editing and retouching. Virtual assistants can help with day-to-day business tasks like scheduling, bookkeeping and communications. You can get ready for expected growth by spending a little time researching options early, so you already know what process to add when you're suddenly slammed with deadlines.

Managing Finances

Financial management is a common reason for business failure in the early years. This business can be so seasonal and being responsible for your own taxes can catch people off guard. What you have in the bank might look great, but it's not really all *your* money. You feel rich, and then you get smacked down by Uncle Sam when he wants his share at the end of the year. You'll also be collecting sales taxes on what you've sold that need to be remitted on a monthly or quarterly basis.

Keep track of Payables. QuickBooks is a great way to note your payables, or what you owe, whether it be taxes, albums, or other products you need to deliver. If you have $10,000 in the bank but you owe $2,000 in taxes, you really only have $8,000. And if you've sold an album for $1,000 and the print lab will charge you $400, you really only have $600. Track payables as they happen and check the balances regularly to get an accurate picture of what you have.

Keep money in reserve. I used to keep an entire separate account for payables. If I sold an album, I would set aside money to cover the expected expenses for delivering that album. When I got paid for a job, I'd deposit the percent of the total that I knew I'd have to pay in income taxes. Keeping those things separate will help you know at a glance how much money you actually have and what you owe.

Save. Save. Save. This industry is very seasonal and cyclical, and there will be downtimes. No matter how successful you become, you will have slow months. Try to build up a 6-month emergency fund, so if you have a slow month or two, you don't have to get a temporary job to cover your bills. Instead, you can invest that time in marketing to bring in more business.

Expect the unexpected. I used to think I knew what to expect. I knew what months would be busy and what months would be lean. When that didn't happen, I'd get stressed. No, capital letters STRESSED. I learned to not take anything for granted. I became a lot happier when I realized I can't predict all the cycles. I learned not to let my foot off the gas, even when business is booming.

Budget. Create a budget that outlines all your costs, including equipment, marketing, insurance, and transportation. If you're paying attention to what money is going out, you'll know when you have to conserve and when you can spend a little more.

Building Your Team

You will probably need help sooner than you think. Continually re-evaluate what you can do yourself and what you need help with.

You might want to add assistants, second shooters, or associate shooters, or hire someone to mange day-to-day communications, or IPS sales. How do you go about it?

1. Identify your needs. Start by evaluating your strengths and weaknesses. Determine the areas where you rock and those where you could use help, as well as what you enjoy versus what you dread. Do you struggle with marketing and client acquisition? Are you overwhelmed by the post-production process? Identifying your needs will help you identify the right individuals to fill those gaps.

2. Define roles and responsibilities. Once you have identified your needs, create clear job descriptions for each role you wish to fill. Whether it's a marketing specialist, an assistant photographer, or an editor, defining their responsibilities will ensure everyone is on the same page and working towards a common goal.

3. Find the right talent. Online forums are a great way to find people, since they typically have experience or interest in the industry. Look for individuals who share your passion, have a solid understanding of the industry, and possess the skills and style that match your needs. And your personalities will need to mesh. I once hired a talented photographer as a second. Based on her talent and effort alone, I would have worked with her more, but that her overall vibe and mine were a real mismatch. It's not like she did anything wrong, I just wouldn't have been able to create a cohesive experience for my clients because our approaches were so different.

4. Communicate. Be clear about your expectations. Let your team know when they do something great, and if necessary help them understand how they can better meet your requirements. Encourage them to let you know what they need as well. You both need to be happy for long-term team success.

5. Nurture and retain talent. Building a team is not just about finding talented individuals; it's also about keeping them motivated and engaged. Offer ongoing training and professional development opportunities, recognize and reward exceptional performance, and create a positive and inclusive work environment that fosters growth and wellbeing.

Building your team is not a onetime task. People will come and go, and your needs may change. But if you can build a strong team, you can set a solid foundation for expanding your business, while also allowing you to focus on what you love most—capturing breathtaking photos and creating lasting memories for your clients.

Making Adjustments

Adjust your pricing at least once a year, and probably every six months for the first couple years. You're quickly gaining experience, and your price may need to increase quickly.

You may need to adjust more than your prices. Look at your sales history. What are people buying? What are they not buying? I've had products I offered routinely because I loved them, but clients

just wouldn't bite. So I took them off my offerings list.
When people are shopping for a photographer, they can get overwhelmed by options, so present only what people are likely to buy.

How do you change prices and still keep your previous clients and their referrals happy? With clients, I will be pretty gentle about raising their prices. I let them know *before* the shoot that the price has increased. For loyal clients, I might even give them one last session at the old price and then tell them it will change next time, so they know what to expect. Don't just send an invoice with an inflated number and ignore it. They might not care about the price increase, but they might feel surprised and disappointed if they get surprised by it, especially if your new price is outside their budget. As your prices increase, you can expect some people to fall off your radar, and at the same time you'll be attracting new clients. That's ok. Your business, your style, and your brand are evolving.

You might get pushback from referrals as well. In the beginning when my prices were changing frequently, I'd have someone call and ask for a booking, and when we talked about the price, they'd say, "But my friend got it for half that! Why is it so much now?" Well, you can't please everyone. Your price is your price. Yet, you have latitude to change your mind. There have been cases when I give a onetime discount to someone because I really want to work with them. There was one wedding where I loved the client and really bonded with the sister of the bride. A couple years later, the sister was planning her wedding, but I had grown out of their price range. Since I knew she was my ideal client type, I told her I'd give a "family" discount (which I made up) because I just wanted to do the wedding. You certainly don't have to, but I like that I can make exceptions when I want to, for the right people.

Taking the Leap from Part Time to Full Time

This can be both the scariest and most exciting moment for a photographer. Are those butterflies or a pit in your stomach? Maybe both. You might feel great about your business, but how do you really know? Is it like when you meet your soulmate and everything just falls into place? Maybe. But it's probably something that you have to put some thought into. Here are some things to consider:

Demand: Are you consistently booking clients and generating enough income to sustain yourself? Is the volume you're booking making it hard to do both photography and your day job? Do you have a steady stream of referrals coming in?

Opportunity: In my case, I went full time when the company I had been working for folded. I found myself with a decision to find another corporate job or make a go of it. Getting laid off is usually considered the worst thing for many people, but for me it turned out to be the universe's version of a mama bird kicking me out of the nest. Is life giving you an opportunity to make a change?

Financial stability: Hoo boy, this is the scary one. There's a big difference between making some fun money on the side and making sure you can cover your bills every month. How much does your household rely on what you contribute? If you're a single-income household or if your income is a big part of your household's needs, I recommend having an emergency fund of 3-6 months of income to help supplement your income while you're growing.

Commitment. Are you willing to invest the time, effort, and resources required to grow a successful business? Is your passion for creating art strong enough to sustain you through the challenges and uncertainties that come with running a full-time business?

Preparation. Have you made sure that you're able to manage every part of this business? That means not just the photography, but all the business aspects, including marketing, accounting, social media, and client communications. You don't have to do it all yourself, you just have to have a strategy, whether it be software, outsourcing, or your own time and effort, for every aspect of the business.

Stepping Up: Instead of completely quitting your day job, is it possible for you to step down to part time in your first months or year of full-time photography? You might go from having a job with a photography side hustle to a photography job with a different side hustle as a stepping stone toward photography being 100% of your income.

Your Mindset: I'll talk about this more in the final chapter of this book. Transitioning to full time will require you to transform yourself into the entrepreneur that will make yourself successful.

How do you know sure if it's the right move? You don't. And you won't. But if you wait to be 100% sure before you take the leap, you probably never will.

Doing Annual Business Tune-Ups

There are a few things you need to re-evaluate every single year to in your quest for long-term success.

1. **Annual reflection. A**t the end of every year I ask myself a few questions. What worked well this year? What didn't work well? Did I achieve the goals I set? What lessons did I learn? Evaluate each aspect of your business, from your pricing to your technical skills, people skills, pricing, marketing, workload, and work/life balance. And for the new year, what are my goals? What do I want to learn this year? What do I want to get better at? What do I want to outsource or automate? If I want to take on new expenses for outsourcing or automating or marketing or advertising, how much additional business do I need to support the cost increase?

2. **Financial Evaluation:** Review your income, expenses, and profits to identify areas of concern or opportunities for growth.

3. **Marketing and Advertising:** Are you attracting the clients you thought you would? If not, there are two things to consider. Is it time for you to change your marketing strategy to draw a different set of clients? Or should you lean in to the successes of the clients you already have and adjust the direction of your business goals? For example, let's say you thought you would be doing a lot of weddings, but you found yourself doing more portraits instead. Does that mean you should adjust your marketing

toward weddings, or adjust your goals to shift toward more portraits? Are your marketing and branding still aligned with your target audience and business goals? Consider the effectiveness of your website, social media, and other promotional materials or advertising. If you're advertising and have gotten zero leads from that source in the past six months to a year, it's probably time to dump it.

4. **Portfolio Review:** Your portfolio needs to be a current reflection of your skills and expertise. Take time to review and update your portfolio with your best and most recent work. This is one of the biggest mistakes I see photographers make. They create their portfolio once and then after a year or two, it's completely outdated. Updating your portfolio means adding your new favorites, but also removing the older images that either aren't as good as your new and improved work, or don't reflect your changing style. Removing images can be hard to do, but you'll need to do it to keep your portfolio from being overwhelming or an inaccurate representation of what people can expect when they hire you.

5. **Continuing Education:** You can't ever stop learning in this field. Whether it's technical skills, expanding your creativity, or refining business techniques, you always need to be improving. Identify areas where you can enhance your skills or learn new techniques. Attend workshops, conferences, or online courses to stay updated on the latest trends and technologies. The investment in professional development will not only improve your craft,

but also set you apart from your competitors. And as an added bonus, money you spend on continuing education can be tax deductible.

Chapter 13
Overcoming Challenges

As much as I have loved my last twenty years in photography, it's not all rainbows and butterflies. Sometimes life is going to smack you in the teeth, and you'll need to deal with it. You'll have critics and haters, and sometimes that person will be *yourself*. I believe the biggest determinant of success is mindset. Not your talent, not your skills, not the software you use or the lists you keep. It's taming the lion of self-doubt and moving forward in a positive way, no matter what life throws at you.

Managing Self-Doubt and Imposter Syndrome

I'm not sure that I know any photographers, no matter how brilliant, that don't deal at times with self-doubt or imposter syndrome from time to time. Especially in the beginning, it's easy to get stuck in feelings of "There's a million amazing photographers out there, why would anyone hire *me?*" It can be some of the hardest parts of this business, especially since there's also a lot of rejection to deal with.

Self-doubt is a natural part of any creative pursuit. The voice inside our heads questions our abilities, compares us to others, and questions whether we truly deserve success. Imposter syndrome is feeling like you're a fraud despite evidence of your competence. They both are natural feelings for creatives, but they can hold you back from moving forward and reaching your full potential. It's easy to say "I'll never get that job, why should I try?"

Here are some strategies for dealing with these feelings when you have them.

- Make a list of what you have accomplished in your business. The items can be big or small, from a list of satisfied clients, to remembering the times you felt proud of moving your business forward, or finding images you're proud of. Remember the day you filed your incorporation paperwork and first felt "official?" How about when you streamlined that workflow to save time? Bam! They don't have to be huge accomplishments. The fact is, it takes a lot of small acts in addition to the large ones to create success. They all are part of the journey, and there's no significant accomplishment that doesn't ride on the back of tiny tasks.

- Keep a record of positive feedback and testimonials from satisfied clients. Read them over when you're questioning yourself. Even when you're just getting started, you've gotten great feedback from friends or clients you've done work for. That initial feedback is probably what gave you the confidence to go pro.

- Don't compare yourself to others. In this field, it's so easy to compare our business to someone else's and think "They're so successful, why am I still scraping by?" As the saying goes, "Comparison is the thief of joy." Someone else's story is none of your business. Your success is about you and you alone.

- Feel gratitude for your wins. A lot of us focus on the negative talk in our head while we dismiss our wins as luck or a fluke rather than a result of our talent and hard work. Gratitude is a starting place for forward progress, and it vibrationally aligns you with the abundance you're moving toward.

- Find meaningful positive affirmations. There are lists of positive affirmations that you can say out loud to yourself when negative thoughts invade your mind. Not all affirmations are meaningful to everyone, so find some that you believe and keep them at the ready.

- Find community. It can help sometimes to just be able to talk with people who understand your challenges. By joining industry groups, attending workshops, or joining online forums, we can connect with others who understand our challenges because they've been there too. Sharing our experiences and learning about others' journeys can provide valuable perspective and ease feelings of isolation.

- Hire a coach. One-on-one or group coaching with a professional can give you tools you need and help keep you focused on what matters. There are coaches that specialize in just about any area of business, including marketing, photography skills, motivation, business processes and organization.

Remember, managing self-doubt and imposter syndrome is an ongoing process. It is normal to have moments of uncertainty, but by implementing these strategies and nurturing a supportive network, we can cultivate the confidence needed to thrive. Embrace your unique artistic vision, believe in your abilities, and allow yourself to grow as an artist and an entrepreneur.

Handling Difficult Situations

No matter how beautiful your photography, how ironclad your contracts, and how impeccable your customer service, you're going to encounter tough situations. There will be difficult clients, you will make mistakes and from time to time you'll experience lean times. How you deal with them can determine the long-term success of your business.

Demanding Clients. Some clients just will try to make you jump through hoops for them. If your expected turnaround time is two weeks, they will ask where their images are in two days. Or maybe you include two revisions for free, but they ask for three, or five, or more. Where and how do you draw the line? First, if you decide to have fees for overages, be specific about them before you start the process. Don't lay a new, unexpected fee on them, even if they are being a tremendous pain. Look at demanding clients as a source of ideas for structures you want to put in place for the future. Also, consider that sometimes people just want to feel special. Sometimes I'll say something like "Well, I'd usually charge for another revision, but if you think we can wrap it up with this last revision, I'll give you this one for free." Or "My usual turnaround is 2 weeks, but for you I'll send a couple sneak peeks tomorrow." You can make them feel special and reward them for working within the limits you set.

Dissatisfied Clients. Hopefully, this doesn't happen often, but it probably will at some point. Maybe a client doesn't like their appearance, or they just aren't happy with the photos for some other reason. This is the toughest part of having a photography business, especially because we can take our work very personally. We want to stand up for ourselves and say, "But I gave you gorgeous images, what's your freakin' problem?" In those rare cases, try to stay humble in your reactions.

I had one client who had a history of hiring very posed, traditional photos. When she hired me, she said she loved that I captured real emotions, and that was what drew her to me. She said she loved how relaxed and happy everyone looked in my portfolio. But when she got her photos, she was disappointed, because they didn't look like the traditionally posed photos she was used to. Even though she hired me because my style was different, she was somehow expecting my images to look like the traditionally posed photos she had before. I realized that what she *thought* she wanted and what she *actually* wanted were two different things. She asked for a refund and I gave it to her, even though I gave her photos that were consistent with my portfolio. I didn't have to give her the refund, but I decided I didn't want her to pay for photos she wasn't happy with, and she appreciated my effort to make her happy. If I had gotten offended or fought with her about contract terms, I would have made the situation worse. You might not choose to give refunds for dissatisfied clients, and you certainly don't have to, but going above what your contract requires can be a way to make the best of a tough situation.

Mistakes and Mishaps. You will make mistakes. As much as I'm compulsively early, there will be rare times when I'm late. And even though I have a stack of charged batteries, there was the time when I had a battery go dead in the middle of a session, and my spare was dead too. Life just happens. When I make a mistake, I try not to merely make up for it, but to go above and beyond. You can offer free products, a free shoot, free retouching, or even send them a gift or flowers. My goal is for the client to almost be thankful for my mistake, because they got something great out of it.

The Threat of Bad Reviews. Some clients will hold you hostage with the threat of a bad review so they can get what they want. I often see this with photographers in conflict with a client. When people do something like this, they're basically bullying to get their way, and it probably doesn't matter what's in your contract, because they likely didn't read the contract in the first place. My philosophy is that when you're dealing with unreasonable people, your best option is to spend as little time with them as possible, which means finding the quickest way to get out of the situation, even if it's not the ideal resolution for you. While you don't have to give in to unreasonable requests, it may be the easiest and quickest way out of a conflict with someone who is determined to be difficult. If you do get a bad review, you can reach out to the platform to get it removed if there's something untruthful in it. And if the platform won't remove it, it's not the end of the world. You can balance out the bad review by asking for more excellent reviews from your happy clients. If you have one bad review and two excellent reviews, it might not look great, but if you have one bad review and 100 great ones, people will see that trend.

Vetting Clients. There are some high-maintenance clients that I know just aren't worth whatever amount of money they would pay. With time, you'll be able to identify the red flags with potential clients. You'll learn to spot difficult people by what they ask for, words they use, or how they talk to you. You don't have to serve those clients. I have turned down clients who I could tell would be demanding from the beginning, or who were a mismatch for my style. You can either tell them you're just not a match, or you can use a simple "sorry, I'm unavailable." It can be really liberating to walk away from potential jobs because you know they will cause you trouble.

Dealing with Competition and Market Saturation

As surely as your grandparents lament that their favorite restaurant has "gone downhill," you'll hear photographers say that the industry is becoming too saturated. People said it twenty years ago when I started, and they say it now. Photography is a very desirable way to make money, so there will always be new people entering the market. Heck, you might be one of them right now. Competition is always part of the picture, but it doesn't need to determine your success or failure. Only you can do that.

Remember, there's something for everyone. Not every photographer is the ideal fit for every client. You need to consider the elements of style, personality, approach, and price, to see that there's something out there for everyone.

The fear of competition comes from a mindset of scarcity, rather than abundance. The fact is that while there are thousands of photographers entering the market every year, many of them won't succeed. Many won't be prepared for what it takes. While the number of competitors in the market is outside your control, it is completely within your control to focus on how you can improve your business and your craft to draw people to you. When you're focused on the abundance that's waiting for you, you can keep your mind occupied by the task at hand rather than the fear of the results.

Half the battle of competition is in your own mind, and that means focusing on making your own business competition-proof, through defining your brand, developing personal relationships with clients and other vendors, continually learning, and delivering consistent quality.

Staying Inspired

You know that saying, "Do what you love and you won't work a day in your life?" It's a load of crap.

We start in this business because we love the craft. We love doing photography, at least the fun, creative, interesting, fulfilling parts of it. But when you do it full time for several years, there will probably come a time when it feels like a "job." You might not do shoots "just for fun" anymore. You might start to enjoy the time away from your camera and computer more than you enjoy the work you're doing. You might not feel the thrill of creation that you once did.

When I find myself losing inspiration in my work, I find it helps to broaden my horizons in photography. I look at the work of other photographers, some who do completely different styles of work than I do. I pay attention to their techniques and see if I could do something similar. Sometimes just trying something new lights a fire.

I also like to explore other genres of art. I get inspiration from films, paintings, art, street murals, sculptures, or even food. I am continually astounded by the unique art created in any medium. I follow art accounts on Instagram and TikTok. I never know when looking at someone's creativity, even if it's not at all related to photography, might make me look at the world differently. Just the other day I saw a play that used color in a unique way, and it got me questioning how I could use those ideas in my photography.

Sometimes, staying inspired might just mean changing up your daily routine a little. Shop in a different store, or go for a walk in a park you've never been to. Sometimes breaking out of your normal routine can shift your energy in a new direction and get you inspired. When I need to shift my energy, I might try shooting something just for fun, using a lens I rarely use, or try a new camera setting, like a different focus mode. You might find a new technique that becomes part of your creative process.

And finally, sometimes staying inspired means taking some time off. At the end of last year, I was shooting nonstop. I was working like crazy, overwhelmed and exhausted, and not feeling inspired. Even vacation didn't reset me. So when January (my off-season) hit, I just needed a break. I didn't pick up my camera for weeks. Then one day I looked at my vase full of Valentine's roses on the counter, seeing the way the light was hitting them, and wanted to shoot again. I ran to pick up my camera and breathed out relief and joy because I was finally feeling the pure love of photography again, just for myself. Taking a break from shooting might be difficult financially, but sometimes it's the best way to give yourself space to recharge.

Finding Work/Life Balance

This is the holy grail, right? Running your own business, kicking ass with your income, and still having the time to actually enjoy life. Is it possible? Burnout is incredibly common in the photography industry. Neglecting your well-being can negatively affect your creativity and long-term business success.

- Establish a schedule. You can set business hours and stick to them. If you want dinner time to be for family, you can make it happen. Set do-not-disturb settings on your phone. Just because someone calls at 9 pm doesn't mean you need to answer it.

- Understand the importance of your own time. I used to worry about posting fun things I did on social media. I figured someone might see me out at a matinee and complain that I had no right to do that when they didn't have their pictures yet. Now I know that as long as I set realistic deadlines and meet them, I can feel confident in taking time for myself.

- Outsource and Automate. If you're continually evaluating your business processes, it will become clear which elements of your business are unnecessary time sucks. When you get them off your plate, you'll have more capacity to step away and take time for yourself.

- Prioritize self-care. Self care isn't selfish. It's necessary. Just like you need to sleep every night in order to have energy and brain power the next day, you need to have downtime in your business if you want to have the energy to work another day. Get a planner and plan the time you need for regular exercise, healthy eating, entertainment and (gasp!) just relaxing.

- Set boundaries with clients. We all will encounter clients who continually demand more and more of us. Clearly communicate your availability and expectations to your clients. Educate them about your work hours and response time, ensuring they understand you value your personal time. Clients that can't respect your boundaries are not good for you.

- Learn to say "No." You might feel like you have to take on every project that comes your way, but you don't. It's ok to say no to projects that don't align with your goals or that require excessive time commitments. It's ok to skip that networking event and take a bubble bath instead. As a business owner, "No" can be so hard to get comfortable with, because we get scared the phone will never ring again. But it will. And you'll be more prepared to take the next job or go to the next event because your mind and soul will be in the right place.

Work/life balance will ebb and flow. You're not going to get it "perfect" because there is no perfect, and there are no rules. What works for you today might not be what you want next month or next year. There will be times when you are happy to put all your energy into the business, and times when you need to scale back to recharge. You can change and adapt as you need. The important thing is to be listening to your heart and your body as it gives you cues.

Chapter 14

Transforming Yourself Into a Thriving Photographer

The fact is, anyone can learn photography. Anyone can learn about aperture, shutter speed, and ISO. Anyone can learn lighting techniques. And anyone can learn how to run a business. It's the unique way that you do all those things that defines your photography business.

It's exciting, really. Being on the cusp of a new chapter in your life. This is your chance to learn and grow both artistically and in your business.

But it's also scary. The fear of failure can paralyze many people. It can keep you from moving forward, or taking chances. You might need to transform yourself and the way you think about things to set yourself up for success. There are a few things that can impede your success:

- Fear of rejection or failure. You might be so worried about failure that it keeps you from taking steps forward.

- Discomfort with uncertainty. You're taking a leap into the unknown, which can be scary.

- Overwhelm. You might be so overwhelmed by how much needs to get done that it's hard to take the first step.

- Confidence. You might question if you're good enough at photography or at business.

- Fear of unintended consequences. You might worry about how doing this will change your life.

The first step toward fixing any of these things is just being clear on what your issues are. I highly recommend finding a coach to help you deal with any of these issues and to keep you accountable and moving forward. It's hard work. Creating a photography business isn't just about the photography, and it isn't just about the business. There's an entire transformation that has to happen to change the doubting version of yourself into the confident, thriving entrepreneur that is your future self. The hardest work you encounter might be the emotional and mindset work that gets you past the blocks that pop up along the way. But that is the most rewarding work. It's the work that will take you from surviving to thriving.

Your Future: The Big Picture

Take a moment to think about your future. Envision your life exactly as you want it to be. What does that look like? How much are you working, and how much are you making? What does your work look like? What does your personal life look like?

If you want that picture to take place, you'll need to draw a line from where you are now to where you will be. Ask yourself questions like:

- What does Future Me know that I don't? How can I learn those things?

- What reputation does the Future Me have in the industry? How can I lay the groundwork for that right now?

- What does Future Me do to take care of themself? Can I create those things up in my life now?

- What does Future Me love about herself? What can I do to develop those qualities?

The Steps to Get There

Now that you have a picture of what you want to create for yourself, you can break it down into elements to get you there. Identify what growth needs to happen. It doesn't even matter if you don't know how to get there yet, as long as you define where you want to go and take steps toward finding out. Move through life as if you're the new, future, better version of yourself.

If you get overwhelmed, break down complex milestones into smaller elements, so that you have manageable tasks you can mark off your list. Give yourself deadlines and reward yourself when you meet them. If you don't meet a goal you set for yourself, be kind to yourself about it. It happens. Don't let disappointment in yourself become a reason to not set other goals.

Identifying Blocks

You might find yourself continually putting off some tasks. Maybe it's something you don't want to do, or something you're afraid to do, or maybe you just don't know what steps you need to take. If you find yourself continually putting something off, you can ask yourself a few questions:

- Do I just dislike doing this task? For me, it's monthly bookkeeping. If that's your block, try setting up a reward for yourself when you're done to make it worthwhile.

- Am I putting it off because I'm afraid? Am I "forgetting" to ask for reviews because I'm afraid they'll be bad? We can get so focused on the bad things that might happen that we forget the risks of not taking action. If you're afraid to do something, consider what will happen if you don't do it. What good things could you be missing out on?

- Am I not getting something done because it isn't "perfect?" Perfectionism can be just a side effect of fear. Fear of getting things wrong. Are you holding yourself back from making progress because you're worried about achieving an unattainable goal of perfection?

- Am I putting something off because I'm not sure what the right decision is? The fact is, we can't ever know If the decisions we make are the "right" ones. Is there a way to test your decision in small ways? Can you play out possible results of each course of action? If you're feeling stuck, remember that not making a decision is actually making a decision. Not wanting to decide may mean you're being drawn toward not making a change.

- Am I listening to my intuition? Sometimes when I'm faced with a task and I feel blocked, I step back to consider if my intuition is telling me it's not the right thing to do. Don't ignore those little whispers that arise as you're moving through your life. If you feel blocked about moving toward something, try to think of alternatives that will make you happier.

Sometimes just having clarity about what is blocking you can help you move toward clearing it. If you become clear about what the block is, even if you don't know the right way to get past it, at least now you'll know what work to do to find out. Awareness is the beginning of transformation. We wouldn't have any answers if we didn't first have questions.

Help With Transformation

You don't have to do this on your own. Whatever phase of your business you're in, someone has been there before. You're not the first to have doubts and questions. You're not the first to have problems. It can help to have the support of people who have been where you are before. Here are some things you can try when you need help:

Find community. There are Facebook groups and industry organizations filled with like-minded people to talk to. Just search for any topic that you need help with and you'll probably find a group of people who want to talk about it.

Find accountability partners. Ask a friend who is also working on a transformation to be accountability partners with you. You might just need periodic check-ins with someone to help keep you moving toward your goals.

Find a coach. There are business coaches, life coaches, and transformation coaches to help you overcome challenges and move toward your goals.

Find resources. You can find books, podcasts, magazines, and even TikTok creators who specialize in any topic, from improving your photography to growing your business or to investing in self care.

Conclusions

The journey from photography hobbyist to professional is one that is filled with countless ups and downs. It requires dedication, perseverance, a constant willingness to learn and grow, and an excitement for the art you can produce. To thrive and not just survive requires reflecting on your actions and ideas in a healthy way so that you can continually grow and improve.

You'll celebrate big wins. You'll produce work you're proud of. You'll make friends. You'll also stumble. You'll make mistakes. You'll have difficult clients, time management challenges, and days when you just don't feel inspired. Between the highs and lows, this can be a rewarding, fun, and lucrative career. Unlike other jobs, you're not depending on someone to give you a promotion. You can make of this career anything you want. You might stay part time forever, or you might build an empire. The results are totally in your hands. "Thriving" is up to you to define.

About the author

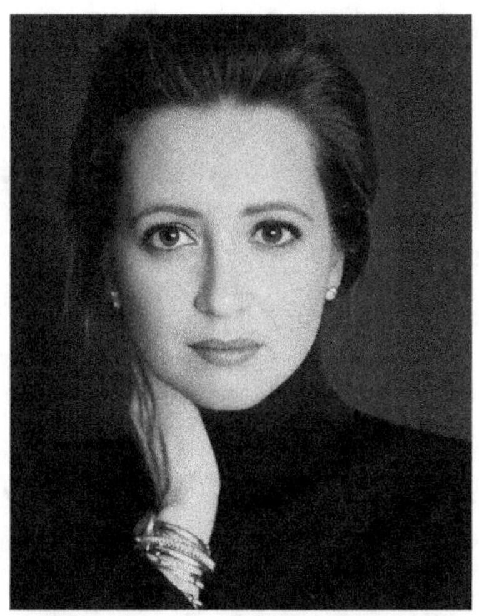

Janet Howard has run a successful 6-figure photography business for the last 20 years. She has photographed over 450 weddings, and thousands of portrait sessions. She is a member of prestigious photography groups Masters of Wedding Photography, World's Best Wedding Photos, and Fearless Photographers. Janet has worked with a variety of celebrities in sports, television and music, and has served companies and brands like Mercedes-Benz, L'Occitane, Jimmy Choo, The Atlanta Falcons, Atlanta United, and The Four Seasons Hotels. Her work has been featured in publications including Vogue, People Magazine, Ebony.com, Vanity Fair, The Knot, Munaluchi Bride, Buzzfeed and HuffPost.

Before making photography her full-time career, Janet thrived in the business world, holding VP-level positions at The Weather Channel and SunTrust Bank, leading teams in technology development and marketing. She has a business degree from the University of Wisconsin, and is a Certified Transformation Life Coach.

After 20 years in photography, shooting over 450 weddings and thousands of portraits, Janet found herself wanting more, offering her experience to help others who want to walk this path.